from
VEDANTA
to
WHATSAPP

Dev Prasad is a senior IT professional currently working in Bengaluru. He has graduated in Electronics and Communication Engineering from NIT Trichy and studied MDP Programme at Indian Institute of Management, Bangalore. He has held senior management positions at various European and American multinational corporations.

His previous three books, *Krishna: A Journey through the Lands & Legends of Krishna*, *Pitch It!* and *The Curse of Surya*, have been bestsellers and have received many prizes and good reviews from the press.

Dev Prasad has been invited to speak on leadership at prestigious forums such as IEEE International Conference, NASSCOM, Rotary Conference, NHRD (Bangalore), NHRD (Hyderabad), TiE, Bangalore Management Association, Madras Management Association, etc. He has also delivered lectures at IIM Bangalore, IIM Ahmedabad, PES University, Jain University, and various top multinational companies.

Dev is passionate about animal rights and working for underprivileged children. He loves cricket, badminton, table tennis and chess.

He can be contacted at dev.prasad63@gmail.com

from
VEDANTA
to
WHATSAPP

#TrendingLifeStories

DEV PRASAD

Published by
Rupa Publications India Pvt. Ltd 2019
7/16, Ansari Road, Daryaganj
New Delhi 110002

Sales Centres:
Allahabad Bengaluru Chennai
Hyderabad Jaipur Kathmandu
Kolkata Mumbai

Copyright © Dev Prasad 2019

The views and opinions expressed in this book are the author's own and
the facts are as reported by him/her which have been verified to the extent
possible, and the publishers are not in any way liable for the same.

All rights reserved.
No part of this publication may be reproduced, transmitted,
or stored in a retrieval system, in any form or by any means,
electronic, mechanical, photocopying, recording or otherwise,
without the prior permission of the publisher.

ISBN: 978-93-5333-447-5

Second impression 2019

10 9 8 7 6 5 4 3 2

The moral right of the author has been asserted.

Printed at Yash Printographics, Noida

This book is sold subject to the condition that it shall not,
by way of trade or otherwise, be lent, resold, hired out, or otherwise
circulated, without the publisher's prior consent, in any form of binding or
cover other than that in which it is published.

The thought manifests as the word;
the word manifests as the deed;
the deed develops into habit;
and habit hardens into character;
So watch the thought and its ways with care,
and let it spring from love.
Born out of concern for all beings.
As the shadow follows the body,
as we think, so we become.
—ANONYMOUS

Contents

Prologue   xi
Introduction   xv

SANKALPA (RESOLUTION)

1. Cheque of Confidence — 2
2. The Coffee Beans Test — 6
3. Defeating Disability — 9
4. Sparky Sparkles — 14
5. The Village Boy — 18
6. Every Burden is a Blessing — 23
7. From Socrates to Steve Jobs — 28
8. Together We Can — 32

AATMABODH (SELF-AWARENESS)

9. The Disfigured Face — 36
10. Inner Value — 41
11. The Foolish Monkey — 44
12. Scars of Love — 48
13. Self-belief — 53
14. Unsolicited Advice — 56
15. The Flawless You — 60
16. Box of Kisses — 64
17. Expand Your Horizons — 67
18. The Real You — 71
19. The Golden Mongoose — 75

KARUNA (EMPATHY)

20. The Grumpy Surgeon — 82
21. Rat Poison — 87
22. Boy in the Ice-cream Parlour — 90
23. The Cookie Thief — 94

24.	The Old Man and His Son	98
25.	Friend or Foe?	102
26.	Humility	106
27.	The Mousetrap	109
28.	Eyes Don't Always See It All	114
29.	Poor Little Rich Man	119
30.	No Pain, No Gain	123
31.	Nail It!	126

SANTUSHTI (CONTENTMENT)

32.	The Three Dolls	132
33.	Nip It the Socrates Way	135
34.	The Muddled Mind	138
35.	How Heavy is Your Glass?	141
36.	Present is a Gift	145
37.	Priorities	150
38.	Peace of Mind	154

KARMA (ACTION)

39.	The Hospital Window	160
40.	The Starfish Story	164
41.	The Race of Life	168
42.	Comfort Zone	171
43.	Kindness	177
44.	What Goes Around Comes Around	181
45.	No Expectations	185
46.	Bridging the Gap	190
47.	Team	194
48.	Take the Plunge	198

NIYATI (DESTINY)

49.	Rat Race	202
50.	A Tale of Two Cats	207
51.	Realizing Your Strengths	211

52. Wheel of Fortune	214
53. Choices	218
54. Second Fiddle	222
55. Sharpen Your Axe	227
56. The House on Fire	232
57. Assumptions	236
58. Team Spirit	239
59. Looking at the Bigger Picture	243
60. Knowledge Without Wisdom	246
Acknowledgements	251
References	252

Prologue

It is nice to be important,
but it is more important to be nice.

—John Templeton

It is true that our ancestors led a more content life than we do. People in earlier times were devoid of many materialistic comforts. Much of what is considered a 'necessity' today was a 'luxury' in those days, and still, we often hear that people in those days were more satisfied with their lives than they are now. People led a more fulfilling life and lifestyle diseases such as high blood pressure, diabetes and cholesterol were either unheard of or known as the 'rich man's disease', as it were mostly they who suffered from these afflictions.

The mindless competition for money, power and glamour has grown exponentially in the past few decades. This phenomenon, aptly termed as 'rat race', has become all-pervasive in the recent times, and today it affects our physical, social and spiritual well-being. For example, during my grandfather's era, most people worked for the government—either in the public sector organizations, the state-owned ones or in the teaching profession. These people had a good 'work-life' balance. By the time my father gained employment, private sector companies were being set up. Along with the private companies came high stress in offices.

During my time, the intense competition and stress began from class XII itself. With thousands of students competing for a few hundred seats at premier educational institutions such as IITs and NITs, one can imagine the stress a student faced.

After graduation, the competition to get into one of the IIMs began. A student with a 98.7 percentile would also not qualify for some of the top IIMs in the country!

The situation has only grown grimmer these days. Competition starts as early as at the age of three when one has to get their child admitted to a good school. The child has to face interviews and excel at other parameters for selection. In some schools, even the parents are not spared. I believe that India is probably the only country where tiny tots applying for kindergarten admission and their guardians have to face such a harrowing experience. The end of education does not signal an end to stress because a high-pressure job soon follows. At every stage in life—whether it is school, college, job or family—a person faces extreme stress.

Last week, I complimented a woman on her son's performance. The boy had secured the first rank in his class. Brushing aside my compliment, she replied dejectedly, 'He got just 98 per cent. I was hoping for more since he is such a bright child.' The young kid is still in VIII standard and the expectations and pressure from his parents are such.

Let us think for a while—is it possible for a person to lead a happy and content life amid all this stress? In many cases, this kind of unhealthy competition leads to deterioration in teamwork, poor interpersonal relationships, and 'politics' in office. These, in turn, have a huge impact on our relationships at home. A person who is unhappy at work cannot lead a content personal life. Similarly, a person unhappy at home can seldom enjoy work.

Have you ever observed the faces of young professionals driving to work each morning? Don't they look worried, tired and hassled? Compare that with the cheerful smiles you see on the faces of vendors in a vegetable market.

Have you noticed people often grimacing in front of their lunch plates in the canteen of a multinational company? Isn't it a sharp contrast to the workers enjoying a packed *dabba* (lunchbox) at a construction site?

Does all this tell you a tale? A few years ago, after experiencing a near-fatal accident, I realized that there was much more to life than cramming for examinations, competing with one's classmates and peers, studying at the top universities, and working for the best multinational companies. The following thoughts keep haunting me every day:

Have you made an impact on others' lives?

Are you winning at the cost of your values and principles?

In the race to win, are you forgetting what you left behind?

Are you able to convert your adversity into success? How high are you on emotional quotient and empathy towards others?

Do you have the ability to look at the bigger picture?

Do you appreciate inner values in others?

Do you know how to live every moment?

What are the traits that are killing you and how are you planning to get rid of them?

Finally, the most important question:

If you were to die tomorrow, how you would like to be remembered? What would you like as your epitaph?

This book tries to answer some of the above questions through a mix of real-life examples and apocryphal anecdotes. It is for those people who are looking for practical wisdom that will help them become more successful, and at the same time, retain their spirituality, cheerfulness, and adaptability. It attempts to awaken your true spiritual self and unleash your infinite potential.

It is never too late to wake up from slumber and change. To quote Swami Vivekananda, 'Arise, awake, and stop not till the goal is achieved.'

Introduction

*I've learned that people will forget what you said,
people will forget what you did,
but people will never forget how you made them feel.*

—Maya Angelou

India is a land of storytelling and storytellers. Storytelling has always been a part of our tradition and rich cultural heritage. The *Ramayana* and *Mahabharata* are two of the greatest ancient epics India gave to the world. These epics chronicle hundreds of stories and anecdotes, and each of them comes with many life lessons.

Indians are not only good at writing stories but also at narrating them. Our parents fondly recollect their childhood days when they would sit on the laps of their grandparents and listen to the enthralling tales of the *Ramayana* and *Mahabharata*.

During the 1980s and the 1990s, Ramanand Sagar's *Ramayana* and B.R. Chopra's *Mahabharata* on national TV had a huge impact on the people of that generation. I vividly remember how, in those days, some banks even changed their timings so that their employees and clients would not miss a chance to watch these epics. In most homes and in public memory, the TV versions of these epics replaced the original ones and the grandmothers of the '90s and 2000s narrated these versions to their grandchildren.

In the last decade, India saw a drastic increase in the number of 'self-help' books by both foreign as well as Indian authors. These books contain stories inspired by the daily lives of ordinary people like you and me. Gradually, these books replaced the great Indian epics as sources of inspiration and motivation.

With the advent of Facebook and WhatsApp, storytelling has assumed a completely different character today. For one, thousands of inspirational stories are now shared on WhatsApp groups. I receive some twenty to twenty-five inspirational quotes and messages every day. I have always wondered how many people genuinely read these messages and more importantly, how many really imbibe and implement them.

Once, I suggested to some of my WhatsApp group members that instead of simply sharing inspirational stories and quotes, we could also share our experiences and narrate to others how that story helped us in our daily lives. For example, if someone shared a message on 'courage', they could also add an anecdote or a personal experience related to it and the lesson they received from it.

Guess what happened next? Nothing! I did not get a single response to my suggestion.

After waiting for three weeks for a response, I doubted if everyone had even read my message. Then, I came across something that confirmed my doubts. The following discussion took place on the group:

Member 1: 'Happy Birthday Anushka!'

In the next ten minutes:

Member 2: Hey Anushka! Many Happy Returns ☺

Member 3: Happy Birthday, girl! How are you celebrating?

Member 4: Have a blast, Anushka!

Member 5: Many Happy Returns, Anushka!

Member 6: Happy Birthday, babe ☺

Member 7: May God bless you dear! Have a wonderful year ahead!

Fifteen minutes later:

Member 1: Oops! Sorry! Anushka doesn't belong here... Wrong group!

I had a hearty laugh. I was now sure that no one seriously read WhatsApp messages. And Facebook fans, don't laugh because you guys are no different! Tell me honestly, among the 100 'likes' that you pressed yesterday on Facebook, how many messages did you genuinely read and like? When you liked and commented, 'Awesome video', did you really watch it until the end? When you liked and commented 'Amazing article', did you genuinely read and understand it? When you liked and commented 'Congratulations', did you actually know what you were wishing the other person for?

Last month, my friend lost his twenty-year-old daughter. The poor girl met with an accident that resulted in her premature death. My friend was shattered. He knew that his daughter had a huge circle of friends, so in order to inform them simultaneously, he posted her photograph on Facebook—mentioning her sad demise. I, too, saw it on my 'newsfeed', and so, I decided to write a condolence message on his post.

When I read the other comments on the post, I was shocked. It had just been an hour since my friend had posted the message and in such a short span of time, seventy-eight friends had 'liked' his message, and around twenty-five of them had posted comments on the photograph:

Your daughter looks so beautiful!
Wow! Cutie!
Beautiful!!!

> Lovely dear…
> When is her wedding?

I posted a message immediately requesting people not to like the post and to avoid writing such comments. I do not think anyone bothered to read my message because a couple of hours later, there were another 100 likes and another twenty-five such comments!

It felt then that this world is not only unfair but also insensitive, heartless, and cruel. But it was not long before I concluded that many people on Facebook don't really read the article that they have liked or commented on. I realized that even though WhatsApp and Facebook are the most popular social media platforms, they are probably not the most effective means to narrate stories or change people's lives. Hence, I abandoned my initial thoughts of telling stories on WhatsApp and Facebook, and decided to express my thoughts with the help of a conventional book.

This book contains inspirational life stories that can change your lives. Though the anecdotes are based on stories borrowed from a wide range of sources—ancient Indian texts to modern social media—they are narrated in my own style and words. Most stories end with my personal experiences, views and a few takeaways.

Sankalpa (Resolution)

Sankalpa is a Sanskrit word meaning 'resolution' or 'determination'. It means possessing good intention. Many of us are not sure about our goals, but to succeed in life, clarity of intention is essential. If the intention is not clear, our attention shifts from one thing to another, leading to confusion and chaos. In such a situation, we often end up compromising our own efforts and receive less than what we actually deserve. Even in times of great stress or adversity, if a person takes a firm decision or *sankalpa* to accomplish a task, he will surely achieve success.

Cheque of Confidence

*All you need in this life is ignorance and confidence,
and then success is sure.*

—Mark Twain

Once there lived a businessman who was reeling under huge losses. His companies were facing bankruptcy and he was continuously flooded with phone calls from various creditors across the country. One day, to get away from the stress for a few minutes and to reflect on his situation, he went to a nearby park. As he sat on a bench, hands over his head, an old man approached him. The old man smiled and asked, 'Why do you look so miserable, my child?'

The businessman did not recognize the stranger. However, seeing the gentle and benign smile on the old man's face, he decided to open up. In the next ten minutes, he quickly explained his woes to him. After listening to the businessman's story, the old man smiled compassionately and said, 'I will help you, my son, don't worry.'

He immediately wrote a cheque and handed it over to the businessman, saying, 'Please take this small contribution from me.'

The businessman was hesitant to accept help from a stranger. Seeing this, the old man gently patted his back and said, 'You can meet me exactly a year later at this very place and repay me.'

The businessman was full of gratitude but before he could thank the old man, he disappeared. The businessman glanced at the cheque—it was $5,00,000! He looked at the signature on the cheque and his eye widened in surprise as he read the name scribbled there. It was signed by Mr John Rockefeller—one of the richest men in the world.

The businessman was thrilled. His first thought was to encash the money and repay all his debts. However, after pondering over it for a couple of days, he decided against it. He kept the cheque safely in a locker and resolved to use it only in case of an emergency.

With a backup, the businessman began to work with an upbeat mood. Having $5,00,000 safely tucked in a locker gave him enough confidence to take a few business risks. Fortunately for him, the risks paid off. He managed to sign a few important contracts. When he received the advance, he invested in better infrastructure and machinery. As the months rolled by, he was able to repay his debts. At the end of seven months, he had repaid all his debts and by the tenth month, he was again making huge amounts of money.

The businessman was a man of principles and he knew he had to repay the amount to the man he had met in the park. On the agreed day, he went to the park with the unused cheque and waited for the old man. Suddenly, out of nowhere, the old man appeared before him. The businessman was thrilled to see him. Just as he was about to hand over the cheque to the old man, a nurse came running.

The nurse held the old man's arm and turned towards the businessman, saying, 'Sir, I hope this old gentleman has not been bothering you. He keeps running away from the asylum and always comes here. He introduces himself as Mr John Rockefeller to everyone.'

Saying this, she led the old man towards the exit of the park.

The businessman stood there, stunned. A mentally ill person had impersonated the richest man in the world and had signed a fake cheque for him, which actually had zero value! And for the last one year, he had taken the biggest risks of his life, confident that he had a backup. He was angry with the old man and his own foolishness. But as moments passed by, an epiphany hit him.

The businessman realized that the entire turnaround of his business, which took place in the last one year, would not have happened had he not believed in the authenticity of the cheque. The cheque had given him self-confidence that had helped him clinch major corporate deals. He understood that having self-confidence was the key to his turnaround and success.

All of us are like that businessman. We are quite likely to take risks in both personal and professional life when we have the comfort of having a backup. I have seen many young engineers quit their jobs and become entrepreneurs. I have also seen people throw away their comfortable jobs to follow their passion. There are also many who give up the corporate world to take a plunge into the social sector. But in most of these cases, they have a strong financial backing—either ancestral property, or inheritance of a fortune, or another family member who is earning enough to take care of their daily needs. There are definitely a few rags-to-riches stories—cases where the person took major risks without any backup, support, or infrastructure. However, such instances are rare.

In the above anecdote, we see that, initially, the businessman was hesitant to take risky decisions even when he faced huge losses. He preferred to make small incremental changes in his daily operations. Making insignificant changes lead to insignificant improvements. If you want to change the fortunes of a company drastically, you must make massive changes in your operating style—something the businessman was reluctant to do.

However, once the businessman received a cheque for a huge sum of money, he had the courage to take calculated risks. He signed many new contracts and invested in infrastructure amongst other things. He began to do everything right and those actions paid rich dividends.

A friend of mine threw a party recently. He had landed a new job that was offering a 50 per cent hike in his salary. He remarked, 'This is my fourth job change. I have noticed something strange about myself. Each time I quit an organization and serve the mandatory three-month notice period, my performance is at its best during that time.'

Everyone laughed.

One of our friends asked, 'How is that possible? When serving the notice period, your interest in your work and loyalty for your company must be at its lowest possible level. How can you say that you give your best performance during such times?'

Recalling the anecdote about Rockefeller and the businessman, I replied, 'When our friend is serving his notice period, his mind is free from any kind of fear. He also does not care about his present job, which in turn, allows him to take bigger risks needed for important decision-making. He is able to soar high because his wings are allowed to flap freely in the wind.'

The Coffee Beans Test

Adaptability is about the powerful difference between adapting to cope and adapting to win.

—Max McKeown

Once a young girl was struggling in her life and sought help from her grandmother. The girl explained her problems to the wise old lady and asked her for a solution.

Without saying a word, the grandmother went into the kitchen and filled three pans with water. She kept each pan on the stove and lit the fire. She put a few carrots in the first pan, a raw egg in the second, and some coffee beans in the third.

When the water in the three pans began to boil, she called her granddaughter. As the granddaughter stood silently in front of the stove, the grandmother emptied the contents of the pans in three different bowls. Then, turning towards her granddaughter, she asked, 'What do you see here?'

The puzzled granddaughter replied, 'Why, just carrots, egg and coffee.'

'Okay. Now touch the carrots and egg and tell me what you feel.'

The granddaughter did as she was told.

'Well...the carrots are soft but the egg is very hard.'

The grandmother handed over the bowl of coffee to her granddaughter and asked, 'And what about this?' The young lady took a sip, closed her eyes and said, 'Hmmm...heavenly!'

The grandmother then smiled and asked, 'Tell me young lady, which one is you?'

Seeing the confused look on her granddaughter's face, the grandmother explained, 'Each of them—the carrots, egg and coffee beans—were subjected to the same conditions. They were kept in a pan of boiling water. However, if you notice, each of them behaved differently.'

The girl replied, 'The carrots that were hard became soft after you put them in boiling water, however, the egg that had a soft yolk hardened after boiling.'

The grandmother replied, 'Yes! And what about the coffee beans?'

'Oh, the coffee tasted wonderful!' exclaimed the granddaughter.

The old lady asked, 'When faced with adversity, how do you respond? Like a carrot, egg or coffee beans?'

In our personal and professional lives, too, we observe different people reacting differently when faced with the same kind of adversity—just like the carrots, egg, and coffee beans.

Many of us exhibit the 'carrot' behaviour. Under normal circumstances, we are strong, but we wilt under pressure. This is a sign of weakness. When faced with adversity, we should become tougher and not give up like the carrot that turns soft in boiling water.

Some of us behave like the egg; we might be soft and fluid like the yolk inside the shell, but we tend to become hard when faced with heat. There are compassionate and gentle people, easy to get along with under normal circumstances. However, the moment they face a problem, their nature undergoes a massive change. They become hard and rigid like a hard-boiled egg.

While discussing the carrot, we concluded that we must become stronger when faced with adversity. Does it mean the egg exhibits the ideal behaviour? No, it does not!

Why not? Doesn't the egg become solid when heated in boiling water? Yes, a boiled egg does give up its softness and becomes tough. However, remember that an egg, when boiled, also loses some of its useful properties. The yolk of a raw egg is soft and fluid. The softness symbolizes kindness in a person. The fluidity indicates the ability to adapt to any circumstances. It also denotes the flexibility to listen to others and change accordingly.

However, the yolk in a boiled egg is hard and becomes a metaphor for insensitivity in a person. The yolk, after coming in contact with hot water, loses its fluidity and becomes rigid—just like an otherwise reasonable and kind person becomes stubborn, someone who refuses to listen to others and sticks to his unyielding views.

The ideal behaviour would be that of the coffee beans. Not only does it change itself but it changes the properties of the hot water too. As the water boils, the coffee beans release their essence into the water. Thanks to the coffee beans, what was once a tasteless liquid now turns into a tasty drink. Under normal circumstances, coffee beans do not possess great taste. However, the moment they are added to hot water, they exhibit their flavour and aroma.

Great leaders behave like coffee beans. They reserve their best for adverse situations. Coffee beans are more effective when put in boiling water, as compared to lukewarm water. Similarly, the more severe the adversity the better is the output of these great leaders.

Defeating Disability

The only disability in life is a bad attitude.

—Scott Hamilton

A German immigrant in the USA, John Augustus Roebling, decided to build a bridge connecting the boroughs of Manhattan and Brooklyn. Considering the technical difficulties involved in executing this project, many experts told him that it would be a foolhardy exercise. Almost everyone had written off Mr Roebling and his dream even before the first design was created.

However, John Roebling was undeterred. He kept dreaming of a beautiful bridge spanning the East River. But he knew he could not do it alone and that his dream had to be shared with others. Since it was a mammoth project, he sought the help of other civil engineers who had expertise in building bridges. Unfortunately, no one was willing to help him. They dubbed it as a 'crazy idea from a crazy man'. Finally, he decided to take help from his son, Washington Roebling, who was an engineer.

The father-son duo worked very hard in putting together a team to construct the bridge. They spent many long nights discussing the bridge's design, the technical challenges involved and the likely solutions.

The project started well, but unfortunately, within a few months, a disaster struck. While conducting a survey, John Roebling injured his foot when a ferry pinned it against a piling. His crushed toes had to be amputated. In a few days, he developed a tetanus infection and died soon after.

The experts once again began voicing their opinion against

the construction of the bridge. However, Washington wanted to keep his father's dream alive and decided to go ahead with his father's ambitious project.

Sadly, for Washington, he suffered a paralysing injury because of Decompression sickness, also known as 'caisson disease'. In the days that followed, this disease also affected many workers. He was unable to walk or talk because of this injury and the subsequent sickness did not allow him to supervise the construction of the bridge.

The cries to stop the construction grew louder. However, Washington did not want to let go of his father's vision. He had the burning desire to fulfil his father's dreams. He rented an apartment close to the construction site, which enabled him to get a view of the work. From his apartment window, he could identify potential problems and correct them.

Washington was greatly aided by his devoted wife, Emily Warren Roebling. She, too, shared her husband's vision and wanted it to be successful. She studied calculations of catenary curves, strengths of various construction materials, specifications of bridges and cable construction. Thus, she became the link between her husband and the workers at the site.

Washington's paralysis restricted his movement to that of just one finger. He came up with a system where he would give instructions to his wife by tapping her with his finger. Then, she would pass on the instructions to the site engineers. For the next thirteen years, Washington kept giving instructions by tapping his finger and his wife kept passing the messages to the construction site!

Today, the Brooklyn Bridge is one of the most spectacular structures built by humankind in the world. It is the first steel-wire-suspension bridge to be constructed. Since its opening in 1883, it has been an icon of New York City and was designated a 'National Historic Landmark' and 'National Historic Civil Engineering Landmark' by the USA.

But the Brooklyn Bridge is not merely an iconic structure, it stands for many other things. It is a tribute to the indomitable spirit of two visionaries and their steely determination. It reminds us of the dedication exhibited by the construction engineers and workers towards realizing the dream of a man and shaping it into reality. It stands for the love and devotion of a wife who, for thirteen long years, kept decoding her husband's messages and helped in the construction of one of the most magnificent structures in the world.

While most of us try to avoid even household chores when we have a minor illness or an injury, these men faced insurmountable disabilities and yet built one of the most magnificent bridges in the world!

How does it feel when one of your limbs is not functioning properly? Frustrating? How does it feel when one is not able to perform basic tasks? Terrible? How does it feel when one is not able to hug their loved ones? Miserable? How is it be to be born without any limbs? It is unimaginable, isn't it?

It is important now to talk about an individual who struggled mentally, emotionally and physically as a child, but eventually came to terms with his disability. At the age of seventeen, he started his own non-profit organization.

Nicholas James or 'Nick' Vujicic, an Australian Christian evangelist, was born with the Tetra-amelia syndrome. This very rare disorder is characterized by the absence of all four limbs. Nick has no hands, and in place of legs, he has small toes.

Nick was born in Melbourne and he spent his childhood in Melbourne and Brisbane, Australia. He struggled physically and mentally as a child. Some insensitive classmates bullied him in school, which made him constantly question the purpose of life.

At the age of eight, he sank into depression, and at the age of ten, he decided to drown himself in the bathtub. However, as he did not want his parents to suffer from the guilt, he stopped himself in the last moment. During his initial years, he was unhappy with God for giving him this disability. However, by the time he turned fifteen, he had come to terms with himself. He was thankful to God for everything that he had.

Nick began to perform his daily tasks—combing his hair, brushing his teeth, using the computer, throwing tennis balls, and even play the drums—using his toes! Despite his handicap, Nick graduated (in accountancy and financial planning) at the age of twenty-one from Griffith University.

At the age of seventeen, what then seemed to be a mundane conversation with a janitor turned his life around. The janitor casually asked Nick to speak to people about his faith in God and the methods he used to overcome his disability. For the next two years, Nick spoke to small groups. At the age of nineteen, he spoke to an audience of around 300 sophomore students. The response was overwhelming and that inspired him to turn this passion into a full-time profession. Over the next few years, Nick travelled across the globe, delivering thousands of speeches in front of vast audiences. His emotional speeches touched the hearts of millions of people around the world. In 1990, he won the 'Australian Young Citizen Award' for his perseverance. Fifteen years later, he was nominated for the 'Young Australian of the Year Award'.

Nothing can be more devastating for parents than to have their child born with a physical or mental disability. The reaction to this condition begins with denial ('I do not believe it, I am sure it is just an ordinary illness, He will be all right soon'), then turns into anger ('Why me?'), and is followed by helplessness ('What should I do?'). Finally, it reaches the stage of acceptance ('Oh, he is fine. All of us are learning to cope with the disability'). In most cases, it ends up with the parents coming to terms with reality—nothing more.

Very few parents go one step ahead and dream big for their differently-abled children. They are content enough if their children are able to lead a normal life. The children, too, resign themselves to leading a life devoid of any challenges and accomplishments.

The anger or frustration is higher among parents who are high-achievers themselves. I remember one of my friends telling me with great anguish, 'My wife and I have been toppers in our class and gold medallists in our respective universities. How can my child suffer from a "learning disability"?' My friend just could not accept the fact that healthy and bright parents could also give birth to a child suffering from a physical or mental disability. It is always better for the child and the parents if they learn to accept their children for the abilities they are endowed with.

When a child is born with a physical disability, it is often assumed that they have a mental disability as well—which is very sad. The child may have deformed hands or legs, but she can easily be the brightest student in the class. Despite being born without limbs, Nick* was able to achieve much more than what most of us can.

---

*Nick is now a very famous motivational speaker and talks mainly on faith, attitude and hope. One of his most memorable quotes is, 'We all make mistakes but none of us are mistakes'.

Sparky Sparkles

The season of failure is the best time for sowing the seeds of success.

—Paramahansa Yogananda

He was the only son of Carl Schulz, a German, and Dena Halverson, a Norwegian. His uncle had named him 'Sparky' after the horse 'Spark Plug' in Billy DeBeck's comic strip.

Sparky struggled throughout his time in school. By the time he had reached grade VIII, he had failed in English, Latin, science, and mathematics, and he was no better at sports.

Sparky was also very shy and an introvert in his early years. He had no social circle and hardly ever dated a girl. In fact, he was too scared to ask due to the fear of rejection. Being mediocre in every activity, he feared the girls would laugh at him. He found solace in the philosophical belief that if someone was meant for him, he would automatically meet her when the time came. This adage helped him to focus on what he did best—draw.

As a child, too, Sparky was very fond of drawing. In school, he submitted his drawings to the yearbook, but faced rejection. Undeterred, he kept going. After completing his school, he got in touch with Walt Disney Studios. They asked him to send a sample of his artwork. Sadly, there, too, he faced rejection. However, by then, Sparky had learnt how to take rejection in his stride—probably because he had gotten used to it.

He began to draw cartoons in which the central character was a 'born loser'. In a way, his cartoons depicted his own life. It served as his autobiography. Slowly, his cartoons began to gain popularity. People began to sympathize with the central character since he was a perennial 'loser'.

This character went on to become one of the most lovable persons in the cartoon world. In a short time, the character became popular as 'Charlie Brown'. Sparky, the young lad who had to overcome constant failures in his early life to create the world-famous 'Charlie Brown', was none other than Charles Schulz.

His cartoon strips *Peanuts* was published daily in 2,600 newspapers in seventy-five countries and twenty-one languages. In the fifty years that *Peanuts* was published, Schulz personally drew nearly 18,000 comic strips!

In the year 1983, 'Camp Snoopy' opened at Knott's Berry Farm, California. This popular amusement park features *Peanuts* characters and has rides designed for young children. In 2000, the Sonoma County Airport was renamed as Charles M. Schulz Airport. The airport's logo sports Snoopy in goggles and a scarf. The Charles M. Schulz Museum and Research Centre in Santa Rosa, opened in 2002, depicts the great cartoonist's life and works. Bronze statues of Charlie Brown and Snoopy have been installed in Santa Rosa.

Schulz received numerous awards during his lifetime. He received the National Cartoonists Society's Humour Comic Strip Award, Society's Elzie Award, Reuben Award, and Milton Caniff Lifetime Achievement Award. For a person who was labelled a failure in sports, he won the Lester Patrick Trophy for his outstanding contribution in the field of hockey and was inducted into the United States Hockey Hall of Fame!

He became a recipient of the Silver Buffalo Award. Subsequently, he was also awarded the Congressional Gold Medal—the highest civilian honour bestowed by the United States Legislature. These are fantastic achievements for a man who had failed in almost all subjects during his schooldays!

One of the key lessons from Charles Schulz's life is that persistence always pays. It is very easy to get discouraged when faced with failure. If it is a case of repeated failures, then it is worse. In this case, Mr Schulz faced repeated failures, and that too, in all walks of life. However, he didn't give up.

❖

We have the habit of judging others by their academic achievements. A class topper is expected to become the most successful professional while a person poor in academics is quickly written off. The reality, however, is completely different. Let me share my own experience.

I had the privilege of studying at the prestigious NIT, Trichy, rated among the top ten engineering colleges in the country. Toppers from various states join this institution, which makes the environment extremely competitive. Electronics and Computer Science are the much sought-after branches there. In Electronics—also my course—there were forty students, and there, too, there were both 'toppers' and people who did poorly. We would speculate amongst ourselves that the 'toppers' would end up as CEOs of blue-chip MNCs while those at the opposite end of the spectrum would struggle all their lives. However, what has happened in the past two decades is unbelievable and unexpected! Most of the 'toppers' have been struggling in their professional careers, while the low rankers are CXOs in their respective organizations.

This is not to belittle one's academic performance. It is just to state that one's academic performance might not have a direct correlation with one's professional success. Apart from talent, it is equally important to have self-belief and a burning desire to follow your dreams. Schulz was fond of drawing cartoons and decided to make a living with that. Even though he faced failures during his schooldays and with Walt Disney Studios, he continued to pursue his dreams. He failed miserably in academics but went on to become one of the most famous cartoonists in the world.

All of us are unique in our own special ways. A person who is poor in academics might be very creative in the field of music and arts, or might excel in sports. Rather than being carried away by mere academic brilliance or the lack of it, we should hone our skills in areas that align with our potential and strengths.

The Village Boy

Do not be afraid of failure; be afraid of petty success.

—Maude Adams

A village boy decided to go to the city to 'make it big'. Like any other village boy, he, too, dreamt of palatial bungalows, expensive cars and a luxurious lifestyle. Little did he know how tough it was to achieve his dreams.

The boy had just enough money to buy a one-way train ticket to Mumbai, the city of dreams. As he came out of the iconic Chhatrapati Shivaji Terminus Railway Station, formerly known as Victoria Terminus, he was awestruck by the skyscrapers around him. Rich men and women were driving around in big flashy cars. Everyone appeared rich. He was convinced that he was in the right place.

For the first couple of days, the boy felt disoriented and lost. There was a huge difference between his village and this big city. He knew almost everyone in his native village and could approach any person and converse with them for hours. He could invite anyone to a nearby tea stall and gossip with him, including the tea stall owner! In his village, life moved at a snail's pace but Mumbai was different. Everyone appeared to be in a hurry. No one had the time to wait and listen to him. Time was money in this city, and who does not love money?

After two days, he ran out of the food his mother had packed for him. He hardly had any money in his pocket. The pangs of hunger drove him to a nearby supermarket in search of a job.

As the boy entered the supermarket, he noticed endless

rows of shelves staring at him. Everyone appeared to be busy picking items off the shelves and loading them into their carts. The boy just stood there and stared at everyone blankly. After observing him for a long time, the manager of the supermarket approached him and asked, 'Could you please tell me what you are looking for? Maybe I can help you.'

The boy was thrilled. Here was someone who had finally volunteered to help him. He replied instantly, 'I am looking for a job. Can you please help me find one?'

The manager laughed. 'Are you new to Mumbai?' he asked.

The young boy nodded and replied, 'I have come from a village which is four hours from here. I am looking for a job.'

The manager asked, 'What have you studied? Are you a graduate? Or a postgraduate?'

These words sounded strange to the village boy. He replied, 'I have studied till X standard,' and added proudly, 'I am the only one in my village who has passed X standard in the last ten years!'

The manager laughed sardonically, 'X standard? Fantastic! May I ask you what kind of job are you looking for?'

The sarcasm was lost on the innocent village boy. With all seriousness, he replied, 'I want to be a storekeeper. A manager. Anything.'

The manager burst into laughter once again. 'Manager, eh? Young man, do you know who I am? I am the store manager. Do you know my qualification? I am a graduate of Bombay University.'

The boy looked dejected. 'You mean I can't get a job here?'

The manager looked at the village boy. He appeared determined and hard-working. He wondered if he could hire him as a helper.

'Would you like to join as a store helper? That's the best

I can offer a boy who has no experience and has just passed Class X.'

The boy replied eagerly, 'When do I start?'

'Write your name, mobile number and email address in the register. I will let you know by this weekend.'

The boy shook his head sorrowfully, 'I don't have a mobile or an email address.'

The manager was shocked. 'You don't even have these basic things? You should perhaps set up a stall and sell fruits!' he said sarcastically.

The innocent boy took the manager's advice seriously. He went to a nearby vegetable warehouse and bought a few kilos of potatoes and onions. Since he had no money to pay, he had to convince the seller to give it on credit.

He came back to the building that housed the supermarket, kept the vegetables on the footpath, and began to call out to people. A few passers-by noticed and approached him. Since the vegetables at the warehouse were not expensive, he could sell them at a neat profit. At the end of the first day, he had made a profit of ₹100. He sold vegetables on the footpath for a few more days.

Slowly, he began to invest his profits in purchasing more vegetables, and very soon, he was able to afford a vegetable cart. The cart allowed him to buy and sell at a faster pace and was thus more profitable. Within no time, he had the money to rent out a small space that would serve as his vegetable shop.

The village boy realized that the cost of cultivation of these vegetable and fruits was very low. The middlemen were taking away most of the profit. He decided to directly buy vegetables and fruits from his own village and transport them to the city. A few years of excellent business helped him in moving from a small vegetable shop to a huge supermarket that sold different kinds of vegetables and fruits.

His rags-to-riches story soon became the talk of the town. Every newspaper, TV and radio channel wanted to interview him. One day, one of India's biggest newspaper company wanted to meet him. Their journalist entered his swanky office and asked him for an appointment.

The village boy, now a young man, smiled at her, 'I am very busy during weekdays. How about this Sunday afternoon?'

The young reporter nodded her head, 'Sure, sir. May I have your email address and mobile number, please? I will send you a reminder on Saturday evening.'

He smiled at her once again and replied, 'I don't have a mobile number or an email address.'

The reporter was shocked. 'Sir, even without them, you have made it so big. Yours is truly a rags-to-riches story. I wonder what you would have achieved if you had a mobile phone and an email address!'

The villager chuckled, 'If I did, I would have probably been working as a helper in some supermarket!'

It is a myth to believe that we can succeed only if we have the best resources. There are many real-life rags-to-riches stories of young boys and girls who sold newspapers in the morning, studied under street lights in the evening, and still succeeded in academics and made it big in business. People with an entrepreneurial mindset are not deterred by lack of funds or resources; their passion, energy and infectious enthusiasm are enough to carry them forward.

In the above anecdote, the village boy did not get demotivated by his lack of education. Neither did he feel humiliated when asked for a mobile number and email address.

Instead of feeling depressed after rejection, he explored new avenues by starting his own business.

Had the village boy followed the normal path of joining the supermarket as a 'store helper', he would not have risen so quickly in his career and would have probably retired as a store manager.

Every Burden is a Blessing

Ultimately, spiritual awareness unfolds when you are flexible, when you are spontaneous, when you are detached, when you are easy on yourself and easy on others.

—Deepak Chopra

There was a farmer who owned an old horse. One day, while grazing in the field, the poor animal fell into an unused well. The horse got scared and began to neigh loudly. Hearing the horse's cries, the farmer ran to the well. Just like any other well, there was no facility to lift a fallen animal. The farmer made a lasso from a coir rope and tried to throw it around the horse's neck and pull it out. Unfortunately, despite several attempts, he failed. He knew that the only option was to seek help from the village headman. Thinking thus, he headed towards the latter's house.

The village headman arrived at the well. He, too, made a few futile attempts to lasso the animal. Finally, with an exasperated sigh, he exclaimed, 'There is no way we can pull him out!'

The farmer asked, 'What do we do?'

The village headman replied nonchalantly, 'We can't save your horse. Let us bury him.'

The farmer was aghast. He exclaimed, 'What?'

The village man explained, 'We will not be able to rescue your horse. He is anyway very old and fragile. I do not think there is much use of having him around. The best we can do is to give him a decent burial for being so useful to you.'

The farmer argued for a little while, but realizing the inevitability of the situation, he finally relented. He knew there was nothing much he could do to save his horse. The village headman was the most knowledgeable and respected man in the village. If he could not help, no one else could.

'How do we bury the horse?' the farmer asked.

Pointing at the loose soil nearby, the village headman replied, 'Let us dig and throw the soil inside the well.'

The farmer nodded his head and went home. A few minutes later, he returned with a couple of spades and buckets. He and the village headman dug the loose mud and filled the bucket with it.

Below, stuck in the well, the horse was getting restless. His cries got louder and more hysterical. Suddenly, he saw a bucketful of mud being thrown at him. Initially, he did not understand what was happening. His master and a stranger were repeatedly throwing mud at him. A few minutes later, the reality dawned upon him. He was being buried in the well! And that too, by his own master, whom he had served so faithfully for all these years.

At first, the horse began to indulge in self-pity. He began recollecting the good years when he was much younger and stronger. He reminisced about the days he had pulled the carriage of the farmer and his family to the nearby town and the time when his master had ridden him across the paddy fields.

As the minutes passed by, the horse found itself being buried in the mud. With each bucketful of mud thrown into the well, the situation was getting worse. The horse knew it was time for action and not self-pity.

Suddenly, with a deep cry of anguish, the horse shook its body. Immediately, the mud on its back fell on the ground of the well. The horse repeated the action and noticed that as the mud fell on the ground, it formed a base, which he could use to lift up his body. He suddenly realized that the mud was no longer its enemy but a friend. Instead of being scared or horrified at the mud thrown at him, he decided to use the situation to his advantage.

For the next few minutes, the farmer and the village headman continued to throw bucketfuls of mud into the well. Each time mud was thrown at him, the horse would shake himself violently. With each shake, the animal rose by a couple of inches. Suddenly, the farmer and the village headman realized what was happening. The farmer screamed, 'Let us continue to throw mud. Looks like my poor animal is going to be saved after all!'

Despite receiving painful blows on his back, the horse decided to continue its fight for life and freedom. A couple of hours later, the well was full of mud. The horse walked out of the well with a triumphant look on his face.

In life, it is important not to be too self-piteous. There are times when our friends turn into foes, and when we think of the times we helped our friends, we sigh painfully, 'How ungrateful he is! Instead of reciprocating my good deeds, he has now turned against me!' This leads us to pity ourselves even more. Instead of reminiscing about the good old days, we should focus on the current situation. How do we tackle the problem at hand? We should also be able to distinguish between a friend and a foe. What seems to be a liability may prove to be an asset. If so, try to use it to your advantage.

In the story, we saw that when the farmer and village headman began to throw mud at him, the horse panicked initially and indulged in self-pity. He viewed each bucketful of mud as his enemy, as a catalyst of his death. As time passed, he realized he would die soon if he did not do anything, and that is when he decided to stop indulging in self-pity and tried to rescue himself.

He realized that he could change this 'agent of death' into a 'guardian angel'. In the end, it was mud, meant to kill him, that saved him.

Once upon a time, an ant was hunting for food. Suddenly, it came across a beautiful multihued feather. Despite the feather being twenty times its size, the ant was not intimidated. It approached the feather to investigate it further. Noticing that the feather was lifeless and dormant, the ant got bolder and decided to carry it home.

As the feather was much bigger and heavier, the ant struggled to carry it during most part of its journey. It had to negotiate several stones and pebbles on its way back home. On a few occasions, the ant dropped the feather. Undaunted, the ant picked it up each time and continued its journey. After a few minutes, the ant reached a crevice.

Here, it faced two problems:

Firstly, how would it cross the intimidating crevice?

Secondly, how would it carry the heavy feather across such a big crack?

The ant pondered for some time, and finally, it had a brainwave! It laid the feather across the crevice and coolly walked over it. After reaching the other side of the crevice, it picked up the feather and continued its arduous journey. After a few minutes, the ant finally reached home. The entrance to its humble residence was a small hole in the field. The ant, once again, laid the feather on the ground. It walked to the end of the feather that was close to the hole. With all its might, it tried to drag the feather into the hole, but because the feather was broader than the entrance to its home, the ant's attempts were futile. After a few attempts, the ant gave up. It abandoned the feather outside the hole and went inside.

This short anecdote has many lessons for us. When the ant first saw the feather, it was neither overawed by its size nor did it see it as a burden. Despite the feather being twenty times bigger and heavier than its own size, the ant decided to carry its beautiful catch along.

When the ant faced a crevice, it was neither worried nor frustrated. It had the presence of mind to put the feather across the crevice and walk over it. This shows us how our burdens, if handled properly, can become our assets.

Finally, when the ant reached home, it was unable to carry the feather inside. It took a few futile attempts for it to realize that it should let go of the feather. This is an excellent lesson in 'detachment'. On numerous occasions, we carry unwanted burdens with us. We are unable to give them up, even if they are detrimental to our well-being. If we learn to be like the horse and the ant, we will not panic during challenging times and adversities. Rather, we will convert our problems into assets and march ahead confidently.

From Socrates to Steve Jobs

Adversity causes some men to break;
others to break records.

—William Arthur Ward

A young man in Greece was struggling in his life. Despite several attempts, he was unable to succeed in any business venture. Frustrated, he sought help from many learned persons. All of them asked him to consult Socrates, the famous Greek philosopher.

The young man approached Socrates and asked him, 'Can you please tell me the secret of success?'

Socrates smiled and replied, 'Please meet me by the river tomorrow morning.'

Puzzled with this cryptic answer, the young man walked away. Next morning, he reached the riverbank at the stipulated time. Socrates was already waiting there for him. The young man greeted Socrates and looked at him expectantly.

'Let us take a stroll in the river,' Socrates suggested.

The young man was sure that Socrates meant 'by the river' and not 'in the river'. However, he realized he was wrong. Socrates held the young man by his arm and began walking into the river.

As they walked deeper into the river, they could feel the water level rise. From knee-deep, it became waist-deep, and soon, it was neck-deep. The young man began to worry because he was not a good swimmer. Suddenly, Socrates caught the young man by his head and ducked him into the water. The young man was flabbergasted to witness this unexpected behaviour from the famous philosopher.

The man did not know how to hold his breath underwater, and soon, he began to gasp for breath. Numerous thoughts crossed his mind. What was Socrates trying to do? Was he trying to kill him? If he died, who would take care of his family? The young man was the sole breadwinner of his family and he could not afford to die.

'There is no way I am going to allow Socrates to kill me,' he thought resolutely. Thinking thus, he used all his force to push Socrates' arm away. As Socrates reeled backwards, the young man swiftly lifted his head out of the water and began breathing normally

'What were you trying to do, huh? Kill me?' screamed the young man.

Socrates smiled and said, 'I was teaching you the secret of success.'

Seeing the puzzled look on the young man's face, Socrates asked him, 'When I held you below the surface of the water, what was the most important thought on your mind?'

Without a moment's hesitation, the young man replied, 'My most absolute desire was to breathe.'

Socrates once again smiled and said, 'And you did it, didn't you? That is the secret of success. When you desire something as much as you desired air to breathe a few minutes ago, you will succeed.'

There are numerous real-life stories of people who turned their lives around when everything seemed lost. There was a time when Apple Computers, due to an onslaught from Windows, was on the verge of bankruptcy. The share markets had written off the company and people were not willing to

join this once-great company. However, Steve Jobs played one of the best 'second innings' of the corporate game. With a series of innovative products such as iMac, iPod, iPhone and iPad, he completely changed the fortune of the bereaved company. At the time of his premature death, Apple had one of the highest market capitalizations among companies in the world of technology.

During the 1983 Cricket World Cup in England, India played Zimbabwe in the qualifying rounds. India batted first, and very quickly, they were reduced to 17 runs for the loss of 5 wickets! The Indian skipper, Kapil Dev, had just arrived at the crease. Within the next 15 overs, he, along with wicketkeeper Syed Kirmani, completely turned the game around. Kapil went on to score 175 runs and it remained the highest ODI score for many years. India won the game and Kapil's knock is considered one of the best ODI knocks in the history of cricket.

While many articles have been written about Apple's turnaround by Steve Jobs and Kapil's hurricane knock in a crucial do-or-die World Cup match, it would be good to study their attitude.

When Steve Jobs began his second innings at Apple Computers, the company was not in the shape he would have liked it to be in. Facing tough competition in the computer market, he realized that minor improvements were not the solution. A fresh approach was needed. Changing the company's name to Apple Inc., Jobs made a foray into the competitive world of consumer electronics. The focus was on innovation rather than renovation. Apple, through highly innovative products, established a brand name for innovation. Ironically, had the situation not been so bad for Apple, he would have probably ended up making small improvements in the computers, and Apple would have been just another computer company.

Under normal circumstances, when a team loses two to three quick wickets, the remaining batsmen play cautiously and steady the ship. The focus is on taking quick ones and twos and not on scoring boundaries. Risks are completely avoided. However, when Kapil was batting at the crease, barring Syed Kirmani, India had lost all its front-line batsmen. With a paltry score of 17 for 5, Kapil knew that taking ones and twos wouldn't help the team's cause. The only solution was to start batting so aggressively that it would cause panic in the opposition camp. That was exactly what he did, and so successfully.

In both these cases, with nowhere to go, the two great men scripted history. Sometimes, we do our best when we are in the most hopeless situation—like a teabag in a cup of hot water.

Together We Can

*We talk a lot about hope, helping, and teamwork.
Our whole message is that we are more powerful together.*

—Victoria Osteen

Once upon a time, a few crows lived on a tree with their young ones. Though the tree was a good nesting place and protected them from sunshine and rain, they had a powerful adversary in the form of a snake.

The snake lived under the tree, and on numerous occasions, it had eaten the eggs or the young ones of the crows. The crows were always sad and anxious because of the existential danger they faced. Hence, they decided to meet the wise owl and seek its advice. Seeing the crows approach him, the owl could sense that something was wrong.

'What brings you all here? What's the matter?' the owl asked.

One of the crows replied, 'Oh wise one, we are worried about our next generation. A snake that lives under our tree eats our eggs and young ones. We have considered leaving the tree multiple times but decided against it, as it is the biggest and the best tree in the neighbourhood. It is the only tree that can accommodate all of us. However, now that things have gone from bad to worse, we have no choice but to leave this tree and find a new home elsewhere.'

The owl replied immediately, 'No! Don't do that. Give me a day, and I will solve your problem.'

Hearing this, the crows flew away with sighs of relief.

There was a huge lake close to the tree. Every morning, a princess would come to the lake with her friends and the women would remove their jewels and bathe in the water. The owl had noticed this daily ritual.

The next morning, the owl flew to the lake and waited for the princess to arrive. Soon, she came with her friends and bodyguards. As usual, the princess and her friends removed their expensive jewellery and kept it on a huge rock. While the guards kept a close watch over the jewels, the girls bathed and played in the lake.

The owl was observing all this from a nearby tree. Then, with one smooth motion, it swooped down, picked up one of the necklaces, and flew away. The guards noticed this and began chasing the owl. Unfortunately, they were no match to the owl's speed. The owl quickly went to the tree where the snake lived and dropped the necklace close to its hole. Hearing the sound of the necklace being dropped, the snake came out of its hole to find out what was happening. Fascinated by the shining necklace, the snake decided to drag it inside its hole to inspect it.

Meanwhile, the security guards, following the owl's trail, arrived at the scene. On seeing the snake holding their dear princess's necklace, they killed it immediately. Then, they picked up the necklace dangling around the dead snake's body and walked away to hand it to the princess.

All the crows once again visited the wise owl and thanked him profusely for solving their problem, and that too, in a day.

There is a famous saying in Hindi, '*Do aur do panch*', which literally means, 'Two plus two is five'. When you add two numbers, the resultant number is greater than the arithmetic sum of the two numbers. Extrapolated, it means that when two entities come together, their combined strength is much more than the sum of their individual strengths.

The above anecdote is a famous story from *Panchatantra*. There is no doubt that snakes are one of the most feared animals by humans and animals alike. It is very difficult for a crow, an owl, or a man to tackle a deadly snake all alone. However, when they worked together, they were able to kill the deadly reptile.

Once, there lived a rich businessman in a village. He had five sons who always fought with each other. The businessman hoped they would mature with age and stop fighting, but unfortunately, things grew worse with time.

One day, he called all his sons. He took ten small sticks and gave two sticks to each of them. He then asked them to break the sticks. Each son could easily break the two sticks given to him. Next, the businessman took ten more sticks and tied them together. He passed on the bundle of sticks to his sons. None of them could break it. It was a lesson in unity for them!

We sometimes fail to understand our own collective strength. Being a cricket lover, I often think of the collective power of a joint Indo-Pak cricket team. Just imagine a cricket team that has a batting lineup consisting of Saeed Anwar, Virender Sehwag, Rahul Dravid, Sachin Tendulkar, V.V.S. Laxman, and the bowling prowess of Waqar Younis, Wasim Akram, Javagal Srinath, and Anil Kumble. Surely, it would be a force to reckon with!

Aatmabodh
(Self-awareness)

Aatmabodh means 'self-awareness' or 'knowledge about one's self'. Only when we develop true awareness of the self, we begin to understand the true nature of the world. We should be careful not to let false knowledge take over our minds and make us either proud or negligent. We should also try to make ourselves aware and vigilant against complacency. Understanding our inner values and goodness is very important. Looks do not and should not matter, as appearances can be deceptive. Everyone is beautiful just the way they are. *Aatmabodh* can help us realize our true worth and find our inner selves.

The Disfigured Face

Love is patient, love is kind, and what our love express is true.
No amount of tragedy can tear, or break the love I have for you.

—Jessica Wheaton

This is a story of a young couple who fell in love. After many years of courtship, they finally decided to get married. Since they wanted an elaborate wedding, they decided to get married five months later to give themselves sufficient time to prepare.

The young man was a soldier. Soon, a war broke out and he was asked to report immediately to Afghanistan. The duration of his stay was unpredictable—it could be anywhere between six months to a couple of years.

Since there was no time for a wedding, the couple had a simple engagement ceremony. It was attended by only a handful of people and was nowhere close to the kind of festivities they had planned. However, the couple was not bothered. They loved each other and that was what really mattered. They held hands throughout the ceremony and hugged each other in the end. The same night, the soldier had to board a military aircraft that would take him thousands of miles away from his sweetheart. Kissing his beautiful fiancée for one final time, he wiped her tears and promised to return soon. They planned to get married as soon as he returned.

Unfortunately, tragedy struck. One fine day, soon after the man left, the woman was driving down a narrow road when she noticed a bike speeding towards her car. She quickly manoeuvred her vehicle towards the right to avoid a crash.

But there was a truck coming at full speed from the opposite direction on that side, which rammed into the car head-on. The girl was immediately rushed to the hospital. She had more than ten broken bones and her internal organs were partially damaged. Her face was disfigured. The doctors did not give her more than twenty-four hours.

However, the young woman was a fighter. She was kept in an induced coma for a week. She survived. Finally, when she opened her eyes, the first thing she noticed was her parents sitting by her bedside. Both her parents were weeping inconsolably. She instantly realized something had gone wrong with her—terribly wrong!

It became apparent to her when she saw her image in the mirror. She had been the most beautiful girl in town and now she was, maybe, the ugliest. Her lovely face was completely covered with scars. Her facial muscles were disfigured, making her look grotesque.

Suddenly, she remembered her fiancé and gradually, her life began to appear in front of her—the courting, the call of the war, the hurriedly arranged engagement ceremony, and then, the accident. Meanwhile, she received many condolence messages from her friends. She ignored them all. The most number of letters came from her fiancé, but she kept all of them aside.

'You must write to him and explain everything that has happened,' her mother begged her.

She ignored her mother's pleas. 'What's the use? He will no longer marry me! Let him marry some other woman and live happily,' she sighed.

After a few requests, her mother stopped. She knew it was no use persuading her reluctant daughter. For the next twelve months, the fiancé's letters continued to pour in—some happy, some sad. He described the war, the deaths, the injuries, and the loneliness. He also wrote occasionally about the food, culture and the people he met. However, none of them evoked a response from her. She would just read them and keep them away in a cupboard. He also called her on numerous occasions, but she never took his calls. She wanted him to forget her.

A year passed. One fine morning, as the young woman lay in her bed, her mother walked in.

'He is here,' she said.

'Who?' asked the daughter.

'Your fiancé,' the mother smiled. If she had hoped to see her daughter elated, she was mistaken.

'Please don't send him inside. Please do not tell him I am here. Ask him to…' Before she could finish, the door opened and a young man in military uniform walked in.

As the soldier walked towards her, the girl tried to cover her face. It was in vain, because he had already seen her.

'I am getting married,' her fiancé happily announced.

The young woman's heart sank. 'This is it! He has come to inform me that he is getting married to the most beautiful girl in town,' she thought to herself. He was dumping her!

Before she could utter a word, the handsome soldier opened his bag and pulled out an envelope. He handed over the envelope to his fiancée, saying, 'That's my wedding invitation. Hope you can make it.'

It was a beautiful envelope. It had a picture of a young couple getting married, surrounded by angels and fairies wishing them. The girl was in tears. Her mind refused to allow her to open the envelope. She looked at her fiancé and asked, 'I am sure you are getting married to a pretty girl?'

Giving a thumbs-up sign, he replied, 'The prettiest in town.'

As the girl turned her face away, he asked, 'Won't you open the envelope?'

Fighting her tears, the girl opened the envelope. She was stunned. She could see her name embossed on the invitation. For a moment, she thought she was imagining it.

She turned towards her fiancé and asked, 'What is this?'

The soldier smiled, 'Didn't I say I am getting married to the most beautiful girl in town?'

The young girl was still confused. 'But I am sure you must have changed your mind…now that you have seen how I look.'

The boy smiled once again, 'No, dear. I was in constant touch with your mother since the past one year. She told me about your terrible accident. She told me about your injuries. She even sent me some pictures of you, taken after the accident.'

'And still?' the girl asked.

The boy replied, 'I loved your beautiful heart. That has not changed. I love you as much as ever.'

Saying this, he gently kissed her. The girl hugged him tightly.

How many of us would have done what the soldier did?

I have known many real-life situations where an intended partner ditched an injured boy or girl. The fiancée or the fiancé was more interested in the partner's appearance and hence could not come to terms with the disfigured face. There are many examples where a girl or a boy left the partner because they no longer found them 'up to their standards'.

This is a real-life example. A boy and a girl were in a steady relationship for many years. The boy was very handsome and every girl's 'prince charming'. The girl's enchanting beauty had made her win beauty pageants not just at the national level but even at the international level. Like all beauty pageant winners, she, too, took a plunge into Bollywood.

In no time, she left her boyfriend of many years, packed her bags, and landed in Mumbai. I was aghast at her behaviour. Though I personally did not know the boy, my heart went out for him.

Sadly, history repeated itself not once but twice! There were two more instances on similar lines—girls winning beauty pageants and becoming overnight celebrities and no longer finding their boyfriend glamorous or having the desired 'celebrity value'.

This happened because the girls gave importance only to the physical looks and status of their partners. The moment they won the international beauty pageants, they decided that their partners were not good enough for them. It is very important to remember that good looks cannot last forever. With passing age, one's physical appearance is bound to deteriorate. The only thing that remains constant is the 'inner beauty'—the heart and soul of a person. If you ever want to fall in love, love the person's inner beauty rather than the physical appearance.

Inner Value

*Your worth consists in what you are
and not in what you have.*

—Thomas A. Edison

A famous speaker was once asked to explain the meaning of inner value in a seminar. He pulled out a beautiful painting and asked the audience, 'Does anyone want this lovely painting?'

Immediately, all hands went up.

Next, he crumpled the painting and asked how many still wanted it. A few hands went down. Not many fancied a crumpled piece of art. Finally, he took the crumpled painting and poured a few drops of tea on it. The painting was immediately disfigured at a few places.

He asked, 'Does anyone still want the painting?'

No one in the audience wanted it.

The speaker next pulled out a 100-rupee note from his wallet and waved it at the audience, 'Who wants this?'

Immediately, all hands went up.

He crumpled the note in his hands and shouted, 'Does anyone still want it?'

All the hands remained raised.

Next, he sprinkled a couple of drops of tea on the 100-rupee note. He then turned towards the audience, 'Does anyone want this crumpled and stained note?'

Once more, all raised their hands.

Then, he dropped the note on the dusty floor and picked it up. He waved the note and remarked, 'This note is not only crumpled and stained but also dirty. I am sure no one would want it in its present condition. However, if there is anyone who still wishes to possess it, kindly let me know.'

Still, all hands in the audience went up.

The speaker smiled, 'Dear friends, I first showed you a beautiful painting that all of you wanted. However, the moment I crumpled it, it lost half its value. Some of you no longer wanted it. When I poured tea over it, none of you wanted it because it completely lost its value. However, your reaction was completely different towards the currency note. All of you wanted the brand new crisp note. Soon, I crumpled it, poured tea on it, and finally made it dirty by dropping it on the floor. Nevertheless, all of you still longed for it. Why? Because its inner value had not changed.'

In our lives, many a times, we are treated like the currency note, aren't we? We are crumpled, stained, thrown on the ground, and sullied. Even then, if we don't become inferior or worthless, it is because our inner value remains unchanged.

Most of the materialistic comforts around us are like the beautiful painting—very precious and good to look at, but a slight damage can completely change its worth and appearance. We hang expensive paintings in our drawing rooms and feel good when it gets appreciation from the guests. However, the moment they are stained or discoloured, we are ashamed to keep them. Either the paintings get shifted to one of the bedrooms or are gifted to the maidservant. Either way, we do not want our esteemed guests to see them!

On the other hand, our soul is like the currency note—it can neither get stained nor can it become impure. There are many saintly people who might not be financially rich. They might wear ragged clothes, and might not even have sufficient food to eat or a proper house to stay in. Despite all the hardships and problems they face, their souls remain pure and clean. They are like the currency note whose value is not diminished.

Do you want to be like the beautiful painting or like the currency note?

The Foolish Monkey

*Do not let what you cannot do
interfere with what you can do.*

—John Wooden

A team of carpenters was working in a temple courtyard in Mysore. They were building a wooden chariot for the upcoming Dussehra celebrations in the historical town. They had been working for the past two months. During the first few days, the carpenters brought logs of wood from the forest and arranged them according to size. In the following few weeks, they began to give shape to the wooden logs. As the festival approached, the logs, under the skilled hands of the carpenters, began to take various shapes like that of chariots, wheels, doors, deities, etc.

A monkey living on a nearby tree had been observing them toiling hard for the past few weeks. The work of the carpenters had stoked his curiosity and he too desired to work hard and help the carpenters.

Every day, the carpenters would go for lunch at 1 p.m. sharp and return by 2 p.m. However, they would ensure that all their tools were locked safely inside the toolkits and bags. This did not allow the monkey any chance to tinker with the tools and try his hand at the woodwork. He, however, patiently waited for an opportunity.

His tenacity paid off when one afternoon, the carpenters forgot to keep the saw inside the toolkit. It lay unattended on the ground. This was an excellent opportunity for the monkey.

He leapt from the tree and landed on the ground.

Once he seized the saw, he began looking around for wood. Unfortunately, there were no logs of wood!

'What should I do? I found a saw but there are no wooden pieces to be cut,' he thought regretfully.

Suddenly, he had an idea. He decided to cut the tree. He took a few leaps and reached the tree in which he resided. He climbed the topmost branch of the tree and sat on it. He realized that the said branch was delicate and hence, it was easier to cut. Thus, sitting on the edge of the branch, he began to cut it with the stolen saw. Meanwhile, the carpenters had finished their lunch and had returned. One of them noticed that the saw was missing.

He shouted, 'Look! Someone stole my saw while we were at lunch.'

'Serves you right for not locking it,' another remarked.

The carpenters began to search the temple premises. Suddenly, one of them looked up and noticed the monkey sitting on the tree. He was busy sawing off the branch which he was sitting on.

The carpenter shouted, 'Look there! A monkey has taken our saw and is sitting on that tree!'

Another carpenter exclaimed, 'If he chops off the branch, he will fall down. Let us stop him from doing so.'

A couple of carpenters ran to the tree and tried to draw the monkey's attention. They threw small pebbles at the busy animal, hoping to make him stop his foolish activity. The monkey thought they were trying to take away the saw from him so he paid no attention to them and continued to saw the tree branch. A few minutes later, the branch was completely sawed off and fell on the ground. The monkey, too, fell with a huge thud. He broke his bones and eventually bled to death.

It is quite common in organizations to find 'juniors' being more hands-on and knowledgeable in the operations and tasks as compared to their 'seniors'. This phenomenon is more acute in today's competitive world with rapidly changing technologies. As you move higher in the hierarchy of an organization, your job is to focus more on the long-term goals of the company and its strategy to achieve them. You are bound to be cut off from operational work. You will definitely drift away from the technical aspects of your work, unless you are working in a hardcore research organization.

The biggest fear that senior managers have is the fear of becoming obsolete. Majority of them do not like to accept that they are technically not on the same level as their team members. The truth is that they need not be. However, this leads to an inferiority complex and their resulting desire to prove their technical knowledge and skills. This problem is more prevalent in companies related to technology. The senior manager also realizes that his subordinates are aware of his deficiencies. He decides to show his knowledge by trying to 'add value' in technical discussions. I have participated in many technical discussions where the agenda of senior management is to merely show off their knowledge. In the bargain, many of them end up cutting a sorry figure. They have probably not heard of the famous adage: 'Better to keep your mouth shut and have people in doubt rather than speak and make people aware of your ignorance.'

In the above anecdote, the monkey had absolutely no clue about the usage of the tools. However, it badly wanted to contribute to making the chariot. It assumed that by sheer observation, it had mastered the art of carpentry. This desire finally led to its death.

A few readers may feel that the monkey was not trying

to show off its carpentry skills but merely trying to help the carpenters. My question to them is: Would you try to help an individual when you are not capable of helping? Let us assume you that find an injured person lying on the ground. Would you attempt to take him in a car if you did not know how to drive, and in the process, kill both—you as well as the injured person? It is always nice to be helpful but not at the cost of causing more harm.

Scars of Love

I think scars are like battle wounds—beautiful, in a way. They show what you've been through and how strong you are for coming out of it.

—Demi Lovato

There lived a young boy with his mother in Kottayam, a beautiful town in the picturesque state of Kerala. Every morning, while his mother cooked for him, the boy would go for a swim in the scenic backwaters that was a stone's throw away from his home.

One day, while cooking in the kitchen, the boy's mother peered through the window. She noticed a horrific sight. A crocodile was swimming towards her son! The crocodile was approaching so stealthily that the boy had no clue of the danger lurking around him. Shocked, the mother ran out of the house. She began to scream as she sprinted towards the backwaters.

Hearing his mother's scream, the boy turned around and noticed a ferocious crocodile close to him. He began to move his legs faster to reach the shore. However, he was no match to the swift and strong crocodile who glided smoothly towards him. Even as the mother continued to shout for help, the crocodile was gaining distance.

A few moments later, the boy managed to reach the shore. Sadly, so did the crocodile. Just as the boy was about to step out of the water, the crocodile grabbed his leg. At that moment, the boy's mother reached the shore and caught hold of her son's hand. The mother began to pull the boy out while the crocodile tried to drag him back into the water. The tug of war continued for a few minutes. The woman was no match for the crocodile's speed, strength and agility. She could slowly feel the boy moving away from her. She was praying desperately to God but it appeared to be a hopelessly one-sided battle between a human and an animal.

A farmer who was passing by heard the woman's frantic screams. He stopped his jeep and looked in the direction of the screams. He noticed the dreadful sight of a small boy held between a tense woman and an angry crocodile. He took his gun and fired a barrage of bullets at the crocodile. He was an expert marksman and hit his target precisely. Hit by a stream of bullets, the crocodile died, immediately releasing the boy from its jaws.

The farmer and the woman picked up the unconscious boy and rushed him to a nearby hospital. The condition of the boy was very critical and his legs were severely injured. The surgeons had to perform a series of surgeries on both his legs. Though the surgeries were successful, they left deep scars on both his legs.

Many TV reporters arrived at the hospital. All of them wanted to interview the young brave lad who had survived such an ordeal. During the course of the interview, the reporters requested the boy to show the scars on his legs. The TV reporters were horror-struck.

The boy simply smiled and said, 'Wait till you see these!' Saying this, he showed them the scars on his arms. The reporters were aghast at the sight, 'Which beast caused you such agony?' one of them asked.

The boy continued to smile, 'These scars are not caused by any wild animal. Nor are they scars of an attack. These were caused by my mother and they are symbols of love.'

'Symbols of love?' the reporter repeated.

The boy explained, 'When the crocodile caught my legs

with its jaws, my mother pulled me with all her might. These deep scars were caused by her fingernails as she held onto me bravely. Had she not held me so tightly, I would have been devoured by the crocodile and would not have been talking to all of you right now!'

❖

A few years ago, I saw a photograph of a young girl in the newspaper. Her face was charred and disfigured. She had just one eye and in the place of the other eye, only burnt skin remained. She had lost considerable amount of hair too. Her lips were torn and teeth broken. It was indeed a shocking sight.

Curiosity got the better of me. I began to read the text below the girl's picture. It was a horrific story. One evening, this young girl missed her usual office bus on her way back home. With no choices left, she waited for a public transport at the bus stop. Since she lived in a remote area, no autorickshaw driver was willing to drop her home. The buses were running full so they did not stop at the bus stop. As the sun began to set and darkness enveloped the surroundings, she became desperate.

Suddenly, she saw a tempo stop by. The driver offered to drop her and asked her to get in. She hesitated because she had heard horror stories about young girls being raped or molested while travelling alone in such a transport.

The driver noticing her hesitation, smiled at her and said, 'Sister, please get in. We are decent people. I will drop you at your doorstep.'

Even as the girl looked unsure, the driver's companion got down and opened the door for her. She slowly entered the tempo and sat beside the driver. A few minutes later, she realized that the driver had suddenly taken a detour and was speeding towards the highway. She asked him about the sudden change in the route, but he just smiled at her.

Soon, he took the vehicle off the highway and drove it into the bushes. As he brought the tempo to a grinding halt, his companion opened the door and pulled the girl out. The two men tore her clothes and raped her repeatedly. The girl fought desperately but she was no match for the two men. She lay exhausted and in a semiconscious state.

After satisfying their lust, the two men decided to burn the girl alive. The driver took a log of wood and tied a ragged cloth to it. Next, he took a petrol can lying in the back of the tempo. He soaked the wooden log with the inflammable liquid. After lighting the log, he marched towards the girl.

The girl slowly opened her eyes. She noticed the rogue move towards her with a glowing wooden log. She tried to run. But unfortunately, the other man caught her with his powerful arms. The duo thrust the lit wooden log in her face, causing heavy damage to her eyes, nose and face. She screamed in agony. The two men laughed at her and continued to torture her. As she fell on the ground, the driver threw the wooden log and indicated to his companion to get inside the tempo. The girl jumped to her feet and took hold of the log. She threw it in the tempo. She aimed in such a way that the log fell straight on the petrol can. The tempo caught fire and within no time, it was reduced to ashes. The driver and his friend tried to get out, but the doors were jammed. They eventually burned to death.

Rescuers found the girl lying in a state of shock. She was immediately rushed to the nearby hospital. Though she survived, her face was full of scars and was badly disfigured. The next day, all newspapers and TV channels carried stories of this braveheart. After reading this story, my eyes were filled with tears. With newfound admiration, I looked at the girl's face once again and silently saluted her.

We should never judge another person's scars because we do not know what caused them. They might be signs of love, affection, torture or even a heroic struggle.

Self-belief

Only when you drink from the river of silence shall you indeed sing.
And when you have reached the mountain top, then you shall
begin to climb. And when the earth shall claim your limbs,
then shall you truly dance.

—Khalil Gibran

There lived a tortoise and two swans near a lake in Bharatpur. There were ample fish and vegetation in and around the lake to provide sufficient food for the trio. However, one monsoon, the rains failed. This led to the vegetation drying up. The reduced water level in the lake resulted in the death of most of the fish. This worried the swans and tortoise.

One of the swans said, 'I think it is time for us to leave this lake and migrate elsewhere.'

The other swan agreed, 'Yes. We will not be able to survive. We should leave immediately.'

The tortoise looked worried. 'What about me?' he asked.

One of the swans replied, 'You should also leave with us.'

The tortoise said mournfully, 'Both of you can fly and cover a few kilometres in no time. I am one of the slowest animals on this planet. Even if I begin to walk right now, it will take me a few months to reach the next lake, and I will surely die in the process.'

Both the swans knew that this was true. They were sad because the tortoise was a good friend and they did not want to lose him. Suddenly, one of the swans had a brainwave.

He told the other swan, 'I have an idea. Let us find a

strong reed or cane. Both of us can hold its ends with our beaks. The tortoise can hold it in the middle with its jaws. Both of us can fly and carry it with us. This way, we will be able to take the tortoise with us.'

The others agreed that it was indeed a great idea. After a quick search, the swans found a suitable cane. They clutched its two ends with their beaks. The tortoise slowly crept near the cane and grabbed its middle.

The swans warned the tortoise, 'Please remember that you're holding the cane with your jaws. Under no circumstances should you open your mouth.'

The tortoise nodded its head. It held onto the cane tightly and the two swans flapped their wings and sailed in the air. A few minutes later, they were flying over a village. A few village boys saw the swans carrying the tortoise.

One of them pointed his finger at them and shouted, 'Friends! Look! What an amazing sight!'

His friends looked at the sky and agreed that it was one of the most incredible sights they had ever seen.

One of the village boys was a sceptic. He said, 'I don't think the tortoise can hold for long. He will soon get tired, relax its grip and fall down.'

The tortoise heard him. He tried to reply, 'Of course not!'

The moment the tortoise opened his mouth, he lost his hold on the cane. He fell down with a thud and died instantly.

There are two lessons one can learn from this anecdote—loss of focus and lack of self-belief eventually leads to failure.

The swans had cautioned the tortoise to hold onto the cane carefully throughout the journey. For the tortoise, this should have been the priority. He should have concentrated only on the task of holding the cane and reaching his destination safely. Unfortunately, the voices from below distracted him, and that ultimately resulted in his death.

It is very important that we do not lose our focus while working on any task no matter how big or small it is. A sudden loss of focus can result in either a delay or a non-accomplishment of the task. Both are not healthy or desirable outcomes.

One of the most important attributes we should have is self-belief. When one of the boys expressed his scepticism, the tortoise should have remained silent. If he had the required self-belief, he would not have opened his mouth to correct the village boy.

In our lives, too, we come across many doubting Thomases—people who are ready to write us off even before we have started our task. The best way to rebuke them is to remain silent and allow our performance to do the talking. When you achieve your results in an emphatic manner, even your worst critic has to eat his words.

Unsolicited Advice

*Many receive advice,
only the wise profit from it.*

—Harper Lee

Once there lived a group of mischievous monkeys on a banyan tree. The winters were very cold because of excessive snowfall and rain. The monkeys found the cold unbearable but they were helpless. They had no means to protect themselves from the severe cold.

One day, the entire region was hit by a ferocious hailstorm. The torrential rains and fierce winds uprooted many plants and trees. A tree adjacent to theirs was uprooted and fell down on the ground with a huge thud. The curious monkeys immediately leapt down from the banyan tree and rushed towards it.

The fallen tree had many fruits. These fruits were very unusual in nature—they glowed like cinders. By the time the monkeys reached the uprooted tree, the sun began to set and darkness engulfed the entire region. In the dim light, the monkeys mistook the fruits for cinders. They pulled the fruits from the branches and began to blow on them, hoping the cinders would glow more and provide heat. However, nothing happened. A bird was watching the proceedings from a nearby tree. He, too, flew towards the uprooted tree and sat on one of its branches.

The bird asked the monkeys, 'Why are you plucking these fruits and blowing on them?'

One of the monkeys replied, 'Don't you know what we

are doing? We are trying to protect ourselves from this cold. It is killing us.'

The bird was puzzled. It asked, 'How do you expect to get rid of cold from these fruits?'

Another monkey replied impatiently, 'You fool! Can't you see these cinders? Don't you know they generate heat?'

The bird laughed loudly. 'Cinders! Cinders!' it repeatedly cackled.

One of the monkeys asked, 'You fool! Why are laughing?'

The bird continued to laugh and replied, 'You are fools, not me! What you are holding in your hands are not cinders, they are fruits. There is no way they are going to glow and generate heat!'

By now, the monkeys were frustrated as none of the cinders were glowing. In addition to this, they had to listen to insults from a silly bird. All of them swooped on the bird and grabbed its wings. They banged it against a hard rock and killed it instantly.

Personally, this anecdote is very close to my heart because of my own experience. A few years ago, when I used to work for a Dutch MNC, I led a huge team of young software engineers. I took it upon myself to mentor them. In my zeal to groom them into good IT professionals, I went overboard on numerous occasions. It started with sharing my own experiences with them and expecting them to internalize it. Initially, it was sporadic and only when sought, but soon I began giving my advice, whether they liked it or not. In my enthusiasm to ensure that they followed my advice, I began to dominate them. Slowly, this turned into a 'my way or the highway' syndrome.

Out of respect for my age, experience and competence, a

majority of my team members were willing to toe my line and I felt happy seeing that. I proudly told my friends that I was grooming young talent in my organization. However, there were also a few exceptions and their recalcitrance caused me a lot of heartburn. They were the ones who were not willing to take my advice. 'How dare they?' I used to think. This not only made me upset but also gave me sleepless nights. I would wake up in the middle of the night and think bitterly, 'I gave this advice to X but he is not willing to do it; I asked Y to temporarily work in this area until I identified a new role but she has quit hastily.'

I became very irritable and short-tempered at work. Though I did not notice it, many of my team members noticed this change in my behaviour. From a jovial manager who would always have fun at work, here I was—all serious, cynical and upset.

One day, one of my team members came to me and asked, 'How about a cup of tea?'

'Sure!' I replied and we headed to the office canteen.

As we were sipping a steaming cup of tea, my team member cleared his throat and spoke, 'You have always allowed me to speak my mind in the past. I feel I can always share the problems openly with you…'

I cut him short abruptly, 'Please come to the point. Explain your problem?'

He smiled, 'Not my problem. Yours…'

I was genuinely surprised, 'Mine? What do you mean? I have no problems!'

Over the next ten minutes, my team member quickly explained his observations regarding my changed behaviour.

I told him the cause for my heartburn and the sleepless nights. He remarked, 'May I ask you a question?'

'Shoot!' I replied instantly.

'Why do you want to play "God"?'

'Play God?' I repeated.

He explained, 'Yes. Though you might be giving advice with noble intentions, it is never a good idea to give advice if it is unsolicited. It has brought you nothing but grief and frustration.' Rather than giving unsolicited advice to everyone, why don't you just give it to those who genuinely ask for it?' he suggested.

I argued, 'Those team members are so immature. I want to groom them and...'

He interrupted, 'That's just your opinion, isn't it? You have assumed that they are immature. You have assumed that they need mentoring. You have assumed that they need you as their mentor, and finally, you have assumed that they should listen to you. Why?'

His words were harsh but had the desired effect on me. For a few minutes, I remained silent. My first reaction was to conclude that my team member was being rude and ungrateful. However, a few minutes later, as my mind became less agitated, I was able to analyze better. I realized that he had spoken the truth—I was indeed trying to 'play God'.

This was a huge lesson for me and my own team member taught it to me.

The Flawless You

I am a perfectionist, so I always feel there's room for improvement.

—Ludacris

This is a story that plays out in Srirangapatna, a small temple town near Mysore. The Ganesh Chaturthi festival was approaching and the king of Mysore wanted to renovate the Ganesh Temple near his palace since it was old and dilapidated. He had instructed his priests to install a new *gopuram* (tower) at the entrance of the temple and paint all the existing pillars and walls. He hired a team of fifty craftsmen to renovate the temple.

The chief sculptor, a master craftsman, was creating an idol of Lord Ganesh. He was a perfectionist. The face of the idol alone had taken him more than five weeks to sculpt. He was in his seventh week and was now working on the limbs. Suddenly, he let out a scream. His fellow craftsmen stopped their work and turned towards him. The sculptor was looking crestfallen. He had clasped his head in dejection. Looking heavenwards, he screamed again.

One of his fellow craftsmen walked up to him and asked, 'What is the matter? Are you feeling sick?'

The sculptor shook his head.

His puzzle colleague asked, 'Then, why did you scream so loudly? Are you in pain?'

The sculptor once again shook his head. His colleague looked at him questioningly.

The sculptor finally spoke, 'We will have to create a fresh idol of Lord Ganesh.'

Everyone was puzzled. The idol was nearing its completion and looked perfectly all right, why was the chief asking to create a fresh idol now? Somebody asked the sculptor for the reason.

The sculptor explained, 'The idol that I was making is damaged. This will not do for the temple. I need to make another flawless piece.'

His colleagues looked at the idol. No one could spot any signs of damage.

A colleague said, 'I don't find anything wrong. Where is it damaged?'

The sculptor pointed towards one of the hands of the deity and said, 'I have chipped off an extra millimetre from the right arm.'

One colleague asked, 'Where is the deity going to be installed?'

The sculptor pointed towards the main entrance of the temple and said, 'The deity will be installed on the *gopuram* at a height of thirty feet.'

His colleagues laughed and shook their heads, 'You are crazy! I cannot notice the damage even when I am standing two feet away from the deity and you are telling me that it will be at installed at a height of thirty feet. Who will notice the flaw from down here?'

The sculptor smiled, 'But I know about the flaw and God knows!'

During my initial years of corporate life, I was busy competing with practically everyone in the organization—not just with my peers but sometimes even with my boss and my own team members. This self-created competition with my colleagues was only elevating my blood pressure and affecting my sleep.

Over the years, as I grew older, I understood the futility of this competition.

I would always keep a tab on my colleagues' activities. I would keep track of everyone's 'arrival' and 'departure' times. I would worry when someone came to the office before me. Similarly, I would wonder why some of my colleagues were staying back late in the office. I would feel very uneasy when I saw any of my peers entering our manager's cabin. If the doors closed, then it made matters worse. What were they discussing? Was my manager planning to promote my peer? Was my peer going to get additional responsibilities?

Such thoughts were destroying me—sadly, the destruction was so subtle I was not even aware of it!

Once I had to undergo medical tests and that proved to be the turning point of my life. I confidently went to the pathology laboratory and gave my samples. The results were shocking! I was suffering from high blood pressure and my sugar levels had breached the upper limit.

While I was busy preparing my new diet plan and a list of 'things to eat' and 'things to not eat', one of my colleagues decided to counsel me. He had worked with me for more than ten years and across two different organizations. My colleague pointed out that most of my flaws arose from a sense of insecurity. He hammered into my head that the only person with whom I should compete was my own self. He said that if I was happy with my quality of work then nothing else mattered. Though I protested initially that he was wrong in his observations, some incidents he narrated made me realize my mistakes.

Over the next few months, I made a conscious effort to change my attitude. To start with, I decided to get out of the 'rate race'. I made a resolution that I would not be bothered about others in the organization and their pace of growth. Since I was not used to this kind of working style, it was quite difficult in the beginning. Slowly, I could sense a change within myself. My next set of medical tests showed remarkable improvement and proved that I was doing the right thing.

In the entire process, I realized that competing with my own self and no one else had two advantages. Firstly, I no longer worried about others' behaviour. I no longer cared about my peers' timings at the office. I was not bothered about their daily life—what they did, whom they met, whom they talked to, etc. Secondly, by competing with myself, I was able to improve my daily work tremendously. I was able to look at the quality of my work, the quality of my deliverables and use them as benchmarks. The next step was to exceed these benchmarks. This way, I was able to constantly challenge myself and raise my own bar of performance. I tried to emulate the sculptor in the temple—the only one who mattered to me, the only one whom I had to satisfy was my own self.

Box of Kisses

Your most precious, valued possessions and your greatest powers are invisible and intangible. No one can take them. You, and you alone, can give them.

—W. Clement Stone

Once, a seven-year-old girl asked her father for ₹20. The father hesitated. He had just lost his job and every rupee mattered. He asked his daughter, 'What do you intend to do with this money?'

The girl smiled and said, 'It is a surprise for you, Daddy!'

The father gave her the money. A few hours later, she came home with a few sheets of gift-wrapping paper. The father was upset. He shouted at the girl for wasting his precious money. The girl left the room crying.

Next morning, the little girl brought a gift-wrapped box for her father and wished him, 'Happy Birthday, Daddy!' The father felt miserable when he noticed that the box was wrapped with the same gift-wrapping paper she had purchased the previous day. He hugged his daughter and thanked her profusely. He felt embarrassed at his earlier behaviour. The girl asked him to open the gift and he did. Imagine his shock when he saw that the box was empty!

Once again, he shouted at his daughter, 'What kind of a gift is this? An empty box? Don't you know a gift box must always contain a present?'

The little girl was in tears. She replied, 'Daddy, the box is not empty. I had blown kisses into the box. I closed it immediately so that my kisses do not escape. I even gift-wrapped them for you, Daddy! It is not an empty box.'

The father felt miserable yet again. He put his arms around his daughter and kissed her lovingly. 'Please forgive me, my child. What an important lesson you have taught me!' he wept.

Years passed. The young girl grew up to become a beautiful woman. She got married and went far away. The daughter and father talked often but seldom met. She could not afford to travel to her hometown and he did not have sufficient resources to travel to her new residence. One day, she received a message that her father had silently passed away in his sleep. The funeral was to be held the next day.

The daughter somehow managed to reach her hometown. A few friends and relatives who had gathered at her house were busy with the funeral preparations. Seeing her father lying in a coffin, she began to sob loudly. She bent down and held his dead face. Tears rolled down her cheeks as she recollected years of her childhood with her father.

Suddenly, the door opened. It was the housekeeper. She stood at the doorway, holding a gift-wrapped box in her hand. The daughter asked her to come in. The housekeeper handed her the box and said, 'Madam, your father always kept this gift-wrapped box under his pillow. Every night he would open the box, blow kisses into it and close the lid. I don't know what it contains.'

Hearing this, the daughter tightly held the gift-wrapped box and said, 'It contains the most precious gems that only a daughter can understand!'

All of us are busy chasing materialistic comforts, and in this chase, we refuse to recognize the kisses of love that our family and friends send us. I work in the field of IT, where I find the majority of the people driven by, and chasing, materialistic comforts. People have little time for anything else.

Long before the IT boom, there was a time when 'loyal' employees were rewarded an HMT watch costing a princely sum of ₹200 rupees by their employers. 'Loyal', back then, meant an employee who had completed twenty-five years in the same organization. All this has changed now.

Nowadays, in many companies, an employee, upon completing three years with the organization, is given one month's salary as the loyalty bonus. Worse still, while making a job change, employees insist on getting a 'joining bonus' from the hiring company.

When technical events are organized in the organization, it is always a challenge to mobilize crowds. In many cases, the young IT engineers are generally not willing to come if there are no 'goodies' thrown in. In one of my previous companies, we conducted 'quality week' to bring awareness of 'product quality' among the employees. We conducted a round of events at our Bengaluru office. The response was quite poor since the young professionals did not feel the need to attend—probably because of the lack of 'goodies'.

A few days later, we repeated this set of events at another location. This time, we were wiser. We decided to have 'spot quizzes' during each event. The winners of these 'spot quizzes' were awarded with ₹1,000 gift cheques. Needless to say, we had close to 100 per cent participation!

In the anecdote about the father and daughter, the former was expecting an object as his birthday gift. When he saw an empty box, he was upset with his daughter. Subsequently, he realized his mistake and felt sorry for his conduct. He immediately apologized to his weeping daughter. Having understood the meaning of true love, he spent the rest of his life blowing kisses into an empty box.

I always believe that children are angels sent by God to teach adults a thing or two. This anecdote just confirms my belief.

Expand Your Horizons

There are many ways of going forward,
but only one way of standing still.

—Franklin D. Roosevelt

Once a gardener lived with his family on the outskirts of a village. He owned a huge nursery consisting of various plants. He took care of his plants lovingly, as if they were his children.

Every week, the gardener would plant fresh seeds in small earthen pots. When the plants grew, he would transplant them to medium-sized pots. As the plants grew bigger in size, he would move them to bigger pots. He enjoyed his mundane task and took great pride in showing off his nursery to his friends and customers.

One day, the gardener received a message from his father. His mother was sick. His father advised him to come home immediately. The gardener hesitated. His parents lived in a remote village, which was around ten hours by bullock cart— the fastest means of travel available to him. He was also aware that his father's village had no proper means of communication with the outside world. When there, he would lose contact with his wife and children. More importantly, he would miss his nursery. He would miss his green babies that grew bigger and became more beautiful with each passing day.

Sensing his reluctance to travel, his wife assured him, 'Please do not worry about us. We can manage by ourselves. Please go ahead and take care of your ailing mother.'

The gardener opened his mouth to speak but suddenly

stopped. Seeing the hesitation on his face, his wife laughed, 'I know what is going on in your mind. You are worried about your plants, aren't you?'

The gardener smiled. How well his wife understood him. How fortunate he was!

He nodded his head, 'Yes, dear. You are right. I am worried about my plants. Who will take care of them?'

His wife patted his arm gently and said, 'Don't worry! We will take care of your plants. The children will help me. Please leave tomorrow morning.'

The next day, the gardener left for his father's village. His wife entrusted the nursery's work to her eldest son. The son looked after the plants with great devotion—just like his father. He ensured that the plants received sufficient sunlight and manure. He fed water to the pots before he ate his food.

Despite the care and love, the plants soon began to wither. Initially, he thought that a few of them were sick. However, as more and more plants continued to wither, he began to panic. He did not have his father to advise him. His mother asked him the reason for his worried look. The boy explained the problem to her. After he had finished showing the sick plants to his mother, she asked him, 'How many times have you transplanted them?'

The boy looked puzzled when he asked, 'Transplanted?'

His mother explained, 'At a regular frequency, you must transplant the young plants into bigger pots. Haven't you observed your father do that?'

The boy said hesitatingly, 'Yes, but...'

'But what?' the mother asked.

'I noticed some of the roots bending and leaves getting spoilt while transplanting. Hence, I thought it was better to leave the plants in the same pot forever,' the boy replied innocently.

The mother took a deep breath and explained, 'As the plant grows bigger, its roots too get bigger and begin to expand. This means that they need more space to grow. This is possible only in bigger pots. Moreover, the stem, branches and leaves, as they too become larger, need more minerals that the soil available in small pots cannot supply. Hence, all plants as they grow need bigger pots that contain more amounts of soil and space. The more we transplant them, the better they grow.'

For the next couple of days, the boy transplanted all the plants from the small pots to bigger pots. He also did not forget to add fresh soil and manure to the plants. Within a week, the withered plants began to look healthy and they gracefully swayed in the wind. The boy was thrilled and hugged his mother.

His mother patted his head and told him, 'My child, always remember that being in your comfort zone may be the most comfortable thing, but it need not be the best thing for one's growth. The plants needed a larger space, more soil and manure. All this was possible only because you kept moving them to newer and bigger pots.'

Just like a plant needs bigger pots and more soil to grow, so do we. If we want to grow in our professional careers, we need to expand our horizons by moving into newer roles and taking up bigger responsibilities. Remaining in the same role can be comforting but it won't allow you to grow professionally.

The boy noticed that when his father transplanted the plants, many leaves and roots got damaged. This was a part of the transplantation process and the young lad failed to understand that. He thought he would damage the plants while shifting them to a new environment.

Aren't most of us like the young boy? Don't we avoid transfers to other cities because we fear that a new city and its environment might damage us? We should understand that the problems that we encounter are a part of our progress and growth. If we are given a higher role in a different city, we should look at the positive aspects rather than getting intimidated. Instead of complaining about the problems encountered in the alien city, we should look at them as challenges and conquer them. In your personal life, too, learn a new language, culture or cuisine. At work, meet your new colleagues, learn in your new role and exceed the expectations set by the management.

The Real You

Some people may fool you for the moment, but be patient. A person's true colours will always show in time.

—Anonymous

Once, in the thick forest of Bandipur, lived a young jackal. The summer season had lasted longer than usual and rainfall that year was scanty. As a result, most of the lakes and ponds in the forest had dried up. This caused great agony to all the animals in the forest.

The young jackal, too, was finding it very difficult to look for food and water. He decided to consult an old wise jackal. The old jackal advised him, 'Son, I know that there is a severe scarcity of food and water in this forest. I strongly advise you to leave this forest and go to the nearby village. Your life will be much better there.'

The young jackal asked, 'Sir, what about you? Will you also join me?'

The old jackal sighed, 'I am too old and weak to travel. I would rather die in this forest. However, you are still young and strong. You must go to the village.'

The young jackal bid him goodbye and left. A few hours later, he reached the village. He was surprised to see so many people there. Most of them were farmers and had cattle, dogs and hens staying with them. As the jackal was walking in a quiet lane, he heard loud barks. He turned around and was shocked to find four dogs sprinting in his direction. Scared, the jackal, too, began to run. A few minutes later, it approached a newly constructed house. The painters were still painting the walls of the house. The scared jackal began to climb the steps of the house. Unfortunately, it missed a step, slipped and fell straight into a huge drum containing blue paint. When the jackal came out of the drum, its entire body was covered with blue paint. The dogs, which were chasing the jackal until then, got scared of the blue-coloured creature. The jackal noticed this. It took a step towards the dogs and they immediately ran away, yelping in fear. The jackal felt happy and he walked towards the marketplace. Many villagers, seeing his blue body, were frightened and they too left it alone and ran away.

Seeing the reactions of the dogs and the villagers, the jackal got an idea. It decided to return to the forest and scare away the other animals. As the jackal entered the forest, the other animals got frightened as well.

'Who is this? What kind of a creature is this?' the lions, tigers, leopards, elephants and deer thought.

They approached the jackal and asked him, 'Who are you? Please tell us from where have you come?'

The jackal spoke with a faux voice, 'I have come from heaven. I am the emperor of all animals. I have descended on earth to rule you.'

All the animals in the forest bowed to the jackal and said, 'Oh Emperor! Welcome to our humble forest. Please stay as long as you wish. Let us know what you wish to eat.'

The jackal asked them to bring sumptuous food thrice a day. The animals, big and small, obeyed him meekly. Despite the drought, they would regularly bring him food.

From that day onwards, the jackal began to enjoy his life. It would spend the entire day sleeping and lazing around in the forest, and when boredom struck, it would scare away some animals for fun.

One full-moon night, all the other jackals of the jungle

had assembled near the lake. Looking at the full moon, they began to howl excitedly. The blue jackal heard the howling of its fellow jackals. Involuntarily, he was gripped by his innate urge to join his fellow jackals. For a while, he resisted but then gave in to the temptation and began to howl loudly.

Hearing the loud howls of the blue creature, all other animals assembled near the lake. For a few moments, they could not figure out who it was, but when they noticed the similarities between the howls of the jackals and their newly appointed emperor, they realized that their divine blue emperor was nothing but a plain jackal!

The lions pounced on the blue jackal and killed him instantly.

❈

Here is another interesting story.

There once lived a farmer in a village in Uttar Pradesh. His village had been facing severe drought since the past few years and his farmland was parched. Since he could not afford an irrigation pump or a borewell, he had been unable to cultivate any crops. Without food or income, he and his family members soon began to starve. He was also unable to take care of his cattle, including his beloved donkey.

This poor farmer had a rich neighbour. The neighbour was able to cultivate crops since he had installed a good irrigation system and had dug a few borewells in his fields. One day, out of desperation, the poor farmer decided to explore the nearby forest in search of some food. He managed to find a few wild fruits for himself and his family. While returning home, he came across a dead tiger. Though the wild animal was dead, the other animals were still scared to go near it. Seeing this, he had a brainwave.

He skinned the dead animal and took the skin home. The next morning, he covered his donkey with the tiger's skin and took him to his neighbour's farm. The donkey moved around the farm, eating the grass and young shoots of the freshly cultivated crops. The neighbour heard the sound of an animal prowling in the farm. He peered outside and noticed a tiger walking around. He got scared and hid himself. This way, the donkey was able to graze fearlessly the entire day!

The next morning, the farmer once again covered the donkey with the tiger's skin and took him to his neighbour's farm. The neighbour was too scared to come out. The donkey grazed happily yet again.

On the third day, when the donkey was grazing in his neighbour's farm, he suddenly heard another donkey braying. Hearing a fellow donkey bray, he too began to bray. The neighbouring farmer, hearing the braying of a donkey in his farm, came out of his house with a huge stick. He recognized the animal prowling in his farm was a donkey disguised as a tiger. He beat the poor donkey black and blue with his stick and killed it.

From both the anecdotes, we understand the importance of being our true self. Like the jackal and the donkey, it is possible to hide our true self and deceive others for a short interval of time. However, ultimately, our true colours show. In both cases, the animals enjoyed a few moments of success but were ultimately beaten to death.

In our interpersonal relationships, too, it is possible to hide our true nature, but only for a short while. It is not long before the mask falls off and we are discovered. It is very important to be honest and it is much better than portraying ourselves as someone different than who we really are and falling off the pedestal one fine day.

The Golden Mongoose

When we become aware of our humility,
we have lost it.

—Anonymous

The Pandavas were victorious at the end of the Kurukshetra war in the *Mahabharata*. After their victory, they marched to Hastinapur and Prince Yudhishthira was rightfully crowned as the king of the massive kingdom of the Kuruvanshis.

Many saints advised the newly coroneted king to perform a yajna to wash away the sins of killing thousands of soldiers during the eighteen-day war. King Yudhishthira, known for his righteousness and respect for holy men, immediately agreed. The yajna conducted by the royal family of Hastinapur was one of the biggest in the century. Thousands of noblemen, princes and kings were invited from neighbouring kingdoms. King Yudhishthira took very good care of all the saints. As a charity, he donated precious stones, gems, gold and silver. Poor and needy people were served sumptuous food for an entire week.

At the end of the yajna, everyone began to praise Yudhishthira for his generosity—saints, noblemen, kings and his subjects. Yudhishthira got carried away by the lavish praises showered on him.

'I am the greatest and most benevolent emperor in the world,' he began to think.

His thoughts were disrupted by a strange noise in the courtyard. He asked his guards to find out the source of the noise.

His guard returned a few minutes later and said, 'Oh Emperor! There is a very strange-looking mongoose in our courtyard and it is behaving in an odd manner.'

Yudhishthira was filled with curiosity. He rushed to the courtyard and found a mongoose rolling on its back. Half of its fur was golden in colour while the other half was grey. It kept rolling on the courtyard and continuously watched its fur—as if it expected something to happen.

Yudhishthira turned to his guards and asked, 'Can anyone tell me why it is behaving so strangely?'

Hearing Yudhishthira speak, the mongoose stopped rolling. He bowed before the emperor and said, 'Oh Yudhishthira, the great emperor of Hastinapur! I have come here to fulfil my desire. Unfortunately, I have not been successful.'

Yudhishthira was surprised to hear a mongoose speak.

He asked, 'What is your desire? Please tell me how I can fulfil it.'

The mongoose narrated a story to Yudhishthira:

There once lived a farmer along with his wife, son, and daughter-in-law. Their village had experienced drought for the fifth consecutive year. Because of this, the farmer had not been able to cultivate any crops in his field. Being a poor farmer, he did not have any borewells or irrigation system and had to depend on Mother Nature.

The drought had forced the farmer and his family to lead a hand-to-mouth existence. They could not even afford to have two proper meals per day. All four of them would beg for food the whole day. At night, they would divide whatever they had been given by the benevolent villagers amongst themselves. Since the drought had affected the entire village, there were not too many affluent people who could give them alms.

One day, between the four of them, they could get just a

handful of rice. The farmer's wife cooked the rice and divided it into four equal portions. They were about to eat when they heard a knock on the door. It was an old beggar and he was begging for food.

Though the farmer and his family members were very poor, they were known for their generosity. The farmer invited the beggar to come inside.

'Please take my share of boiled rice and satisfy your hunger,' said the farmer and handed over his plate to the beggar.

The beggar quickly ate the farmer's share of rice and looked around hungrily.

The farmer's wife said, 'I can't eat without my husband. Let me hand over my share to you.'

The beggar happily ate her share too, but he was still not satisfied.

The farmer's son said, 'It is my duty to follow my parents' footsteps. I would like to hand over my portion of rice to you.'

Saying this, he too handed over his plate of rice to the old man.

The daughter-in-law, watching all this, said, 'I cannot eat my share when my whole family is fasting. I also notice that you look famished, so kindly take my share as well.'

The moment the beggar had finished everyone's share of boiled rice, there was huge thunder and lightning.

A divine voice said, 'Oh farmer! I had heard a lot about your generosity and I was just testing you! I am Lord Indra, King of Gods. I am very happy with you and I will reward your suitably.'

At that time, the mongoose was nearing the farmer's hut, hunting for food. His body touched a few grains of rice that had fallen on the floor. Immediately, that part of his body became golden in colour. However, the other part of his body retained his original colour. The mongoose asked Lord Indra, 'Oh Lord! Half my body is of golden hue. Please tell me how to make my entire body gold.'

Lord Indra replied, 'The generosity of this poor farmer converted your fur into gold. Unfortunately, your fur touched the grains only on one side of the body. You should search and find an equally generous person on earth. When you rub your body on his food, your remaining fur too will become golden.'

The mongoose finished telling his story and looked at Yudhishthira, 'Oh Emperor Yudhishthira! Since the past few months, I have been visiting the homes of rich men and rolling myself in their dining area. Unfortunately, none of them have been as generous as the poor farmer, and therefore, my fur didn't turn gold. One of my friends told me that you are performing the biggest yajna in the world, and I decided to visit your courtyard and rub myself on the food morsels lying on the floor. Unfortunately, though you are known for generosity, you are no match for the poor farmer. I have to go back disappointed.'

Saying this, the mongoose disappeared in a flash. Yudhishthira was bewildered. He had never had such an experience in his life. His bloated ego was ruptured. His looked at his brothers. All of them were equally shocked and remained silent.

Yudhishthira looked at Lord Krishna and begged with folded hands, 'Oh Lord! You know everything. Please tell me what this is. I thought I was the most generous person on earth, but I am evidently not.'

Lord Krishna smiled, 'Oh Yudhishthira! Though you are the epitome of truthfulness and righteousness, I had noticed that your ego had bloated by the end of your yajna. You began to believe that you were the greatest person on earth. I requested Lord Yama to come in the form of a mongoose and teach you some humility.'

Yudhishthira understood everything. He bowed in front of Lord Krishna and begged for forgiveness.

There is a Yudhishthira among all of us, is there not? Even the most humble person swells with pride when he is donating his wealth, clothes, or food to needy people. Though there is nothing wrong with feeling good when doing it, we should always remain grounded. It is nice to be benevolent and generous but it is equally important to remember that our action does not make us any greater than the person receiving our generosity. Among all the traits that a person should have, humility is one of the most important attributes. You might be the most intelligent, richest or the most generous person in the world, but if you do not have humility, you have nothing at all!

Karuna
(Empathy)

Pragya (wisdom) and *karuna* (empathy) are two sides of the same coin. When you begin to see yourself in others and empathize with them genuinely, you will find that they too reciprocate those feelings. Being warm and sensitive towards people, understanding them, and being compassionate brings positivity and happiness. Empathy is about being in someone else's shoes, that is seeing with his or her eyes and feeling with his or her heart. *Karuna* begets karuna and it helps in nurturing relationships.

The Grumpy Surgeon

Empathy is really the opposite of spiritual meanness. It is the capacity to understand that every war is both won and lost. And that someone else's pain is as meaningful as your own.

—Barbara Kingsolver

A young man had a major road accident. While trying to avoid a speeding truck approaching from the opposite direction, he ended up encountering a head-on collision. The road was narrow and that had made the crash almost inevitable. He was immediately rushed to a nearby hospital.

His father was informed of the ghastly accident and within minutes, he reached the emergency ward of the hospital. The nurses had just wheeled his son into the operation theatre. While the junior doctors were busy moving in and out of the operation theatre, the surgeon was nowhere to be seen. The father was restless. He repeatedly asked the nurses about the absence of the surgeon. The nurses calmly replied that the surgeon was on his way. Finally, the surgeon arrived at the scene. He quickly changed his clothes and headed towards the operation theatre.

'What took you so long? Don't you know my son's life is in danger?' the father barked.

The surgeon replied calmly, 'I was not in the hospital. I was stuck at another place and needed time to drive to the hospital. As you know, the traffic is bad during these hours. Please calm down.'

The father shouted, 'Calm down? My son is critical and you expect me to calm down? You are a surgeon and I guess you see hundreds of such cases every day. This is just one more case for you. Had it been your own son lying wounded here, would you have replied in the same way?'

The surgeon replied, 'Doctors can just do their duty. Do you know who heals? It is He who heals. Pray to Him.'

Saying this, he pointed at a picture of Lord Ganesh mounted on the door of the operation theatre.

Hearing this, the father calmed down a bit. He muttered something about speeding up the operation and saving his son. But by that time, the surgeon had already disappeared into the operation theatre. The father touched the picture and prayed to God. He prayed for the next few hours.

Finally, the door of the operation theatre opened. The doctor removed his headgear and mask. Seeing the boy's father, he said happily, 'Phew! That was a close one! I am glad that he was operated on time. He is saved.'

The boy's father was relieved. As he opened his mouth to speak, the doctor waved at him, 'If you have any questions, ask the nurse.'

Saying this, he removed his green apron, threw it in the cupboard, and sprinted across the corridor. The boy's father approached a nurse and said angrily, 'I am yet to meet a more arrogant person in my life. This is supposed to be a noble profession. The doctors are supposed to treat their patients and respond to queries. Look at him rushing out of the corridor.'

A teary-eyed nurse replied, 'Sir, the surgeon's son died a few hours ago in a road accident. No one could save him. When your son was brought in, we called him immediately. He was performing the final rites at his funeral. Hence, there was a delay from his side. He dashed off immediately after your son's operation because he needs to collect his son's ashes at the crematorium.'

Hearing this, the boy's father collapsed.

All of us have this nasty habit of judging people based on our limited perceptions rather than looking deep into reality. In this anecdote, the injured boy's father was restless and tense at the hospital. His worry was aggravated by the surgeon's absence. Rather than giving the surgeon some benefit of doubt, he assumed that the surgeon was negligent.

After the surgery, the doctor had to rush to collect his son's ashes at the cremation ground. Once again, the boy's father failed to empathize with his hurried departure. He attributed the doctor's brief reply to being arrogant and rude. There are numerous occasions where we run into our friends at supermarkets, malls or restaurants. At times, they may be in a hurry to meet another person. They might even be rushing for an important appointment. But our immediate thoughts are: 'X has become so arrogant!' or 'What does X think of himself?' or 'Doesn't X have even a minute to spare for me?'

We conclude, 'X has changed so much since I last met him!'

Isn't it strange that we dub a person as arrogant or haughty based on just one data point, despite having known him for so many years? If we are ready to write off an old friend based on one unusual incident, how will we react if a total stranger exhibits similar behaviour?

Many years ago, as a teenager, I suffered from dust allergy. I took treatments from many doctors, but all was in vain. My friend, who had a similar problem, recommended me to meet a doctor—let us call him Dr X.

Dr X was one of the most renowned doctors in this

field. Despite having taken an appointment, we had to wait for more than a couple of hours. When my turn came, my mother accompanied me inside. My mother began to tell him my entire medical history. The doctor cut her short and said that he wanted to examine me.

Throughout the doctor's examination of my lungs, throat and nose, my mother kept chatting. The doctor took no notice of her. My mother was offended. Finally, the doctor wrote a prescription and said there was nothing to worry about. My mother asked the most common question that any patient's mother would ask, 'Doctor, when should I bring my son again for a check-up?'

The doctor got up from his seat, opened the door for us, and replied, 'You need not come back. It's not needed.'

Saying thus, he asked the receptionist to send the next patient inside. My mother was flabbergasted! She could not believe what had just happened.

'How dare he speak so rudely to me?' she said angrily.

I replied, 'Oh come on! Didn't you notice his clinic is swarming with patients? He is a very busy doctor.'

'I am old enough to be his mother!' she retorted.

I chose to remain silent.

'Did you hear his reply at the end? When I asked him about our next visit, he responded rudely and said that we need not meet him,' she continued.

'But isn't that good? Isn't that a sign of his confidence in his treatment?' I argued. Noticing my mother's glare, I explained, 'Isn't it every patient's dream to not visit the doctor again?'

My mother was not convinced by my logic. She constantly questioned the doctor's competency. However, I took the doctor's medicines faithfully, and within a few weeks, I was cured of an ailment that I had been suffering from for many years.

A few months later, I overheard my mother telling her friends about the incident. I couldn't resist adding, 'And the doctor was wonderful. Just as he had predicted, I just needed one course of medicine. I was cured without a second visit.'

This incident had a huge impact on my mother. She changed her opinion about the doctor completely. It was also a lesson for her to be more objective, rather than making hasty conclusions. The next time someone exhibits a seemingly rude or indifferent behaviour, it might be beneficial to assume that the person may have valid reasons for doing so.

Rat Poison

Forgiveness is not always easy. At times, it feels more painful than the wound we suffered, to forgive the one that inflicted it. And yet, there is no peace without forgiveness.

—Marianne Williamson

Once, a farmer lived with his wife and three-year-old son. Their house was in a farm infested with rats. One day, the farmer handed a bottle to his wife and said, 'This bottle contains rat poison. Please put a few drops in all the crevices of our house. That's the only solution to kill these rats.'

The wife immediately began executing the task. By the evening, she had covered all the holes and crevices of her home. The bottle was half-empty. The next morning, as the farmer was leaving the house, he noticed the bottle with its lid open. Since he was in a hurry, he requested his wife to put the lid on the bottle and keep it safely away from their son. His wife, busy in the kitchen at that time, promised to do it after she was done with the cooking. Unfortunately, she got preoccupied with other household chores and completely forgot to close the bottle.

Meanwhile, the little boy saw the bottle lying on the floor. Mistaking the purple liquid for grape juice, he drank the rat poison. Within a few minutes, he collapsed on the floor. His mother noticed him lying unconscious and immediately rushed him to a nearby hospital. The doctors tried their best but, sadly, they could not save the boy. The boy's mother was devastated. Along with the sadness of losing her child, she was also scared.

How was she going to face her husband? What was she going to tell him? What would be his reaction?

Within a few minutes, her husband arrived at the hospital. He looked at his dead son and approached his wife. She was scared to even look into his eyes. As she began to move away from him, he ran and hugged her tightly, weeping and saying, 'I love you!'

The wife was stunned. She had not expected this kind of behaviour from her husband. Rather than scolding her for her negligence, he was expressing his love. As the wife looked puzzled, the husband said, 'There is no point blaming you for our son's death. I know how busy you are during the day. In the midst of cooking food, taking care of our son and doing all the household chores, it is quite natural that you might miss a few things. It is my fault too. Rather than instructing you to close the bottle, I should have done it myself.'

The husband realized that there was no point in blaming his wife. Having lost their only child, she was as distraught as him. There was no use driving home the same point at the time of pain and loss. What she really needed then was someone to help her get rid of her guilt and shower her with love and affection.

How would we have reacted if we were in this man's position? Angry? Frustrated? Helpless?

In our personal and professional lives, when things go wrong, we spend too much time in finding the root cause and blaming the culprit. Rather than lending support, our entire focus is on expressing our ire on the individual. When the man reached the hospital and saw his dead son, he knew the root cause very well. He guessed that his wife had forgotten to close the lid of the bottle even after he had instructed her to do so immediately.

In a normal situation, the man would have shouted at his

wife, blaming her for the loss of their son. He would have probably told her, 'I had given you strict instructions to close the bottle. However, you neglected it. Look what it has caused! You are to be blamed for this!'

Hearing this, the wife, already grieving about their lost child, would have gone into severe depression. She would have been ridden with guilt for the rest of her life.

'Oh! What have I done! I have killed my only child,' she would have repented.

However, instead, the husband was empathetic towards his wife. He realized that since she had numerous household chores in the morning, it was quite natural for her to forget to follow his instructions. He also realized his own blunder. Being aware of the contents of the bottle, he should have just spent an extra minute at home and closed the lid of the bottle, rather than rushing to work.

Here, it would be worthwhile to indulge in introspection and think of our own empathy quotient. Would we have sympathized with the wife and absolved her of the blame for the child's death? Would we have the courage to accept our own mistake?

Ultimately, it is all about forgiving others, having the ability to 'let go', and thinking of the future. Once the damage is done, there is little use grieving over it. It is imperative to 'let go' of the past and ensure that a similar situation does not occur with you or with any of your loved ones in the future.

Boy in the Ice-cream Parlour

*The nobler a man,
the harder it is for him to suspect inferiority in others.*

—Marcus Tullius Cicero

A boy walked into an ice-cream parlour and sat at a table. A waiter soon arrived and asked him his for his order. The boy wanted to eat a triple sundae and asked him the price of the same.

The waiter replied, 'That will cost you ₹200.'

The boy put his hand in his pocket and pulled out all the notes. He asked the waiter, 'How much does a fruit salad with ice cream cost?'

The waiter replied, 'Same price.'

With a dejected face, he asked the waiter, 'How much does an ordinary chocolate ice cream cost?'

The waiter was getting irritated. It was a Saturday evening and the ice-cream parlour was full of impatient customers unwilling to wait. And here was a boy asking for the price of all the flavours available in the ice-cream parlour!

The waiter rudely replied, '₹190.'

The boy's face lit up.

'I will have that,' he replied immediately.

A few minutes later, the waiter brought the ice cream and kept it in front of the boy. He also kept the bill for ₹190 and walked away. The boy silently ate the ice cream, relishing every bit of it. After finishing it, he paid the amount at the cash counter and left the ice-cream parlour.

A few minutes later, the waiter returned to clean the table.

Tears filled in his eyes as he saw two ₹5 coins kept next to the empty cup—his tip!

He ran out to thank the boy, but unfortunately, his little customer had already left. The boy had exactly two hundred rupees so he did not want to purchase an ice cream which cost the same amount as that would not allow him to tip the waiter. For the boy, tipping the waiter was as important as eating the ice cream itself, hence, he kept asking the rates of different types of ice cream. He wanted to ensure that he had sufficient money for the tip.

Unfortunately, the waiter behaved just the way a majority of us would have behaved. He began getting impatient with the young customer. Probably for two reasons—firstly, because it was peak hour and the place was swarming with customers, and secondly, because he did not think that a small boy, who was counting his money, was a lucrative customer. 'Let me serve a few rich customers who can tip me better' might have been the thought in his mind.

In our lives too, don't we all draw conclusions about other people without having sufficient knowledge about their situation? Don't we judge the intentions of others based solely on our preconceived notions?

Here is another interesting anecdote, which involves the former World Chess Champion, Viswanathan Anand. This incident took place much before the smartphone era—at a time when people on a train used to talk to their co-passengers rather than browse intently on their mobile phones.

Once, Anand was travelling by rail. His co-passenger started a conversation with him, by asking him the most common question, 'What do you do?'

Anand promptly replied, 'I am a chess player.'

The man smiled, 'Yes, that's nice to know. But what do you do?'

Anand smiled back and said, 'I am a chess player and I do that full time.'

The man was shocked. He further questioned, 'Don't you plan to go to college? Don't you want to work?'

Anand confidently replied, 'No, I am planning to make a living with it.'

The man advised him, 'Young man, sports is a very unpredictable career, especially in India. Only if you are Viswanathan Anand can you probably make a living by playing chess, otherwise, I wouldn't advise you to pursue that.'

Anand just smiled.

When I first read this, I did not believe it. How did you react?

Did you laugh at the man's stupidity?

Did you get angry with the man for undermining his illustrious co-passenger?

Did you admire Anand for his humility?

Well, I had all the above reactions. However, after some retrospection, I realized that the man's behaviour was quite normal. Ninety per cent of people would have behaved in a similar manner. Don't we have this habit of typecasting and sizing up other people?

The moment the man saw a middle-class-looking co-passenger travelling in a train, he assumed that this person was struggling in life, forget about thinking that he could be a celebrity. I am curious to know how the co-passenger would have reacted if this conversation would have happened in the first-class section of an aircraft.

We see similar behaviour in the ice cream anecdote too.

The waiter assumed that the young boy who was counting his money in the ice-cream parlour must be hard pressed for cash; that he did not have sufficient money to buy an ice cream for himself, let alone leave a generous tip.

These two anecdotes teach us the perils of typecasting people with our limited knowledge. We should never draw any conclusion until we have sufficient information about the other individual.

The Cookie Thief

I always feel that life can teach you how to act. I am looking at life through other people's eyes. By feeling empathy. And I do feel that I am constantly learning.

—Cara Delevingne

A woman had a very early morning flight to catch. She decided to arrive at the airport the previous night itself and wait in the departure lounge. Since she had many hours before her flight, she decided to buy a book and something to eat. After purchasing a novel and a bag of cookies, she settled down in a nearby chair.

Soon, she was engrossed in her novel. A few minutes later, she heard a soft rustling sound. She noticed a middle-aged bald man sitting one seat away from her. This person was opening the bag of cookies lying on the chair between them and taking cookies from it! As the woman watched in shock, the man helped himself with a couple of cookies. The lady was too taken aback to react. She was angry but decided to remain silent. She was not interested in creating a scene over a couple of cookies in front of the other passengers.

She, however, decided to put her hand inside the cookie bag and took out a couple of cookies for herself in order to send a message to the thief that she was the one who owned the bag of cookies. The man, hearing the rustle of the packet, looked at her and saw her taking out the cookies but he merely gave her a smile and an approving nod. The man's shameless behaviour infuriated the woman. But she controlled herself.

A few minutes later, the man dipped his hand once again

and helped himself with a few more cookies. Not to be outdone, the lady, too, grabbed a few cookies. She was furious as she watched her neighbour deplete the stock of cookies in the bag. But she still chose to remain silent. Finally, there was just one cookie left in the bag. He took the last cookie and broke it into two pieces. He offered her one of the pieces.

'The audacity!' she thought as she grabbed the piece of cookie from him. The bald man just smiled at her. She was getting impatient and kept looking at her watch. Whenever, she would turn towards her neighbour, he would give her a cheerful smile. Seeing her neighbour's brash demeanour, she was further irritated. Here she was, fuming and cursing him, and he, on the other hand, was smiling, guilt-free and trying to be friendly with her!

Finally, her flight number was announced. She heaved a sigh of relief and began to leave hurriedly. Pushing the empty cookie bag towards her neighbour, she stood up and picked up her luggage. She expected her neighbour to thank her for the cookies but he did not utter a word.

'Ingrate thief!' she cursed as she headed towards the air bridge. Once seated in the aircraft, she was happy to get rid of the horrible company she had at the airport and decided to finish her novel to take her mind off the experience. As she opened her bag, she almost screamed. Right in front of her eyes was her bag of cookies! It took her a few minutes to let everything sink in. If her bag of cookies had been with her all along, whose cookie bag had she eaten from?

Soon, she realized that she was the cookie-thief! All this while, she had been shamelessly eating cookies from her neighbour's bag and cursing him for nothing. In reality, she was the one who did not have the courtesy to thank her cheerful neighbour for his cookies!

As her aircraft took off, she realized it was too late to apologize. She neither knew the man's name nor his address. With a deep sigh, she turned to her right. She exclaimed with joy when she discovered that her neighbour was once again the same bald man! With a huge smile, she offered him her bag of cookies.

❖

In this story, the woman wrongly assumed that her co-passenger was a thief. But she had no evidence to support this thought. Since she had just purchased a bag of cookies, her immediate assumption was that the bag lying nearby was hers—an incorrect supposition.

Does this not happen with us all the time? Don't we all make assumptions about others and draw our own conclusions? The woman got a second chance to make amends, but with most of us, it is too late by the time we realize the truth. Often, we end up hurting others or ourselves by our behaviour.

Think about what happens when the woman of the house loses a piece of jewellery. Who is invariably the prime suspect? Isn't it the maidservant? What happens when the man of the house loses something in the car? Isn't the driver automatically deemed the culprit?

This is in a way linked to the earlier anecdotes about Viswanathan Anand and the boy ordering ice cream. In both those examples, 'the other person' was assumed inferior. This anecdote is the result of assumptions stemming from the thought: 'If the other person is inferior then he must be the guilty person.'

How do we avoid such situations in our daily life?

To begin with, we should never jump to hasty conclusions. It is equally important to give the benefit of doubt to the other person. When the woman of the house loses an earring, why doesn't she think of all the possibilities? She probably misplaced it and forgot about where she had kept it. She probably lent it to a friend and is unable to recall. Perhaps, her daughter took it without informing the mother. The possibilities are endless.

Similarly, when a person loses an object in the car, there are many likely scenarios. It probably fell under the seat and remained hidden from the view. His child might have noticed it and picked it up. It might have accidentally fallen off somewhere else.

The next time you suspect or accuse someone of theft or wrongdoing without an iota of clear evidence, please remember the cookie story!

The Old Man and His Son

*Love is that condition in which the happiness of
another person is essential to your own.*

—Robert A. Heinlein

An old man was terribly sick. He knew that he was going to die soon. His last wish was to meet his only son who was serving in the army. He conveyed his wish to the doctors who agreed to inform his son immediately. In the evening, there was a gentle knock on his hospital room's door. The nurse opened it. Standing at the door was a handsome young man dressed in an army uniform.

The nurse heaved a sigh of relief. 'I am so glad you could make it. I don't know how long he will live,' she whispered. Holding the military man's arm, she led him into the room.

'Your son has arrived,' she announced to the old man lying on the hospital bed.

The old man strained his eyes. He noticed a young man in an army uniform standing before him. He held out his hand. The military officer clasped it tightly and assured him, 'Don't worry. I am here to take care of you.'

Saying this, the military man pulled a chair nearby and sat down. Hours passed. The young man held the dying man's fragile hand and spoke to him soothingly. He expressed his love and gave him encouragement. Around midnight, the nurse entered the room. She noticed that the scene had not changed at all. The young person was still sitting on a chair next to the patient—holding his arm and speaking to him occasionally. The dying man hardly spoke.

She asked the young man, 'Would you like to sleep? Shall I organize a bed for you?'

The military officer politely refused and said he preferred to sit next to the old man. As the first rays of sunlight entered the room, the old man died in his sleep. The military man released the lifeless hand and informed the nurse. The nurse had been taking care of the old man for two years. During this time, she had become quite close to him. She felt like a daughter who had lost an ailing father. She could very well imagine how the son was feeling.

Turning towards the military man, she said, 'Sir, I am so sorry that he died. The only good thing was that he could meet you.'

The young man asked, 'Who was this person?'

The nurse was shocked. She replied angrily, 'He was your father, young man! How can you be so inconsiderate?'

The young man replied, 'Oh no. I have never met him. I don't know who he is.'

The nurse was puzzled, 'Then why did you come inside and spend the whole night with him? If he was a stranger to you, why didn't you say so?'

He replied, 'I had come to the hospital to meet a friend. I entered the wrong room. As soon as I walked inside, I knew it was a mistake. I realized that the dying man was waiting for his son. It took me just a few seconds to know that the old man had poor eyesight. I also knew that his son had not arrived. He was probably fighting in a battle. Since I knew that he did not have much time, I stayed back as his son.'

In the above anecdote, the military man came to the hospital to meet his friend. Despite entering the wrong room, he stayed back with the old man—a total stranger. He realized that the need of the stranger was far greater than the need of his friend.

It is quite natural to see people helping their relatives, friends, and acquaintances. Parents help their children, and in turn, when the parents grow old, their children take care of them. We help our friends in need. We support our relatives in the time of crisis. But how many of us would be ready to help a total stranger?

Let us imagine for a moment, you are driving from Mumbai to Pune through the Western Ghats. You notice a car which has broken down. The person trying to repair the car looks like one of your friends. You immediately apply the brakes, halt your car and switch off your engine. You rush towards your friend to help him fix his car. As you approach him, you realize that this person is not a friend but a complete stranger! A case of mistaken identity!

What will you do? Will you still go ahead and help him—thereby delaying your arrival in Pune? There is a high chance that you might tell him that you had just come to inspect the problem, give him a few suggestions and return to your car. How will the struggling stranger feel? He will experience the entire gamut of emotions—from a sense of relief on seeing a stranger approach him to a feeling of disappointment. Déjà vu?

In the Bhagavad Gita, Lord Krishna explains to Arjuna that all of us are independent souls and the concept of relationships is a myth. A person who is your father or a son in this life may have been a complete stranger in your previous life. Similarly, your mother or daughter in this life may be a stranger in your next life. With this knowledge in mind, one should realize that there is no one who can be truly termed as a 'stranger' or a 'friend' or a 'relative'.

All of us have come from the same source and after death, we will return to the very same source. In a way, we are all strangers, and in another way, we are all brothers and sisters.

So, why not help each other when in need?

Friend or Foe?

To suspect a friend is worse than to be deceived by him.

—Francois Duc de la Rochefoucauld

On a late night, a businessman was heading home. It had been a hectic and miserable day for him. His deliveries had been delayed and hence he had to face the wrath of many customers. Many important people in his business had taken leave and this had further aggravated the situation. It wasn't going well for him at the home front as well. His borewell pump had broken down. The milkman and the maidservant had not come and his driver had reported sick, so he had to drive back home from work. He was longing to reach home, take a shower, have a quick dinner and retire to bed. His aching body desperately needed some rest.

The businessman's office was in Lonavala and his house was located in the nearby hill station of Khandala. Both these quaint towns are on the picturesque Western Ghats. Though this gave him an opportunity to admire the charming hills during the drive, it also meant he had to accost tough hairpin bends on the roads.

The most difficult part of the drive from Lonavala to Khandala was the absence of any street lights on the highway. Any good driver had to rely more on instincts than on visibility. As the businessman was negotiating one of the steep curves, he noticed a truck coming from the opposite direction. Watching the truck driver's rash driving, the businessman cursed under his breath, 'Another drunken driver. Nothing new. Half the truck drivers seem to be under the influence of alcohol these days!'

The truck sped past him swiftly and just missed hitting his car. As the truck crossed him, the truck driver stuck his neck out and screamed at him, 'Buffalo!' This behaviour of the driver was the last straw for the businessman. He, too, stuck his head out and growled at the truck driver, 'You pig!'

The truck driver's shout had awakened the sleeping beast in him. After calling him names, he pressed his accelerator fiercely and sped ahead at a frantic speed. As he took a sharp turn, his car banged into a huge buffalo that was sitting right in the centre of the highway!

This is a classic case of misinterpreting the situation and misjudging the intentions of others. The truck driver had noticed a huge buffalo in the middle of the highway. Like most buffaloes, this one was also a gentle beast, standing, oblivious to the traffic zipping across the highway. The truck driver had narrowly missed hitting the animal, which, due to its dark colour, was not visible in the darkness of the night. He did not want others to face a similar situation and thought it was his duty to warn the fellow travellers. When he saw the businessman's car coming from the opposite direction, he tried his best to warn him.

Unfortunately, the businessman misinterpreted his warning as an abuse. He continued to speed on the highway and soon met with a serious accident. When things go wrong, we always curse our ill luck, seldom realising that the early warnings are always right in front of our eyes. Why do we find it so difficult to differentiate a friend from a foe? If a person says or does something unusual, why do we immediately brand him as an enemy rather than analysing the situation?

Once, a bird was flying across Himachal Pradesh. It was during the winter season and was extremely cold. After flying for a few kilometres, the poor bird could no longer take on the gusty winds that blew across the hills and fell down on the ground. As it lay shivering, it heard a cow approach him.

The bird was thrilled. It thought that the cow would save it. It tried to scream to draw the cow's attention. Unfortunately, it was weary and weak. It was unable to scream loud enough to catch the cow's attention. The cow dropped some dung on it and walked away.

'How dare the cow drop its dung on me?' the bird thought angrily.

It tried to get up from the dung but was unable to do so. As it lay on the ground, it realized after a while that the cow dung was actually keeping it warm. It was no longer shivering in the biting cold. Though it seemed like the cow had humiliated him, in reality, it had indirectly done him a huge favour.

After a couple of hours, the bird was feeling sufficiently warm and it began to sing with joy. A farm cat heard the bird singing and came near it. Initially, it was unable to see the bird. However, as its sharp ears followed the sound, it found the bird buried in a pile of cow dung. The cat pounced on the bird and pulled him out. The bird thought it was finally out of the dung and could now fly away. But before the bird could realize what was happening, the cat killed him and gobbled him up!

It is important to note that when the cow dropped its dung on the bird, the latter immediately assumed the cow to be its enemy. He felt angry and humiliated to have dung dropped all over him. He was cursing the cow for its arrogant behaviour. However, a few minutes of staying in the warmth of the cow dung was enough to change the bird's mind. Similarly, the bird was initially happy to see the cat approach the dung. However, its joy was short-lived. It had wrongly interpreted the cat as its saviour.

A person watching the scene above would have also initially concluded that the cat was helping the bird by removing it from a pile of cow dung. It appeared to be a friend. However, the cat's evil intentions were soon exposed. It had pulled out the bird only to devour him.

We experience such situations in our daily life too. People who seem harmful to us may actually help us, without us realizing the same. It is similar to the driver on the highway and the cow in the field. So, the next time someone shouts at you, he might actually be helping you!

Humility

Fighting means you could lose.
Bullying means you can't.
A bully wants to beat somebody;
he doesn't want to fight somebody.

—Andrew Vachss

Once there lived a family of sparrows in a huge banyan tree. The big tree provided ample shade and a resting place for the sparrows. It was situated near a lake.

One hot afternoon, an elephant came to the lake to quench its thirst. After drinking water, he walked towards the banyan tree and started shaking the tree's branches playfully. The sparrows got worried. They had built numerous nests on the branches of the tree. A strong shake from the elephant meant the nests would fall on the ground. The sparrows flew to the elephant and bowed before him.

They said, 'Oh, mighty one! Please stop shaking the branches. Our nests will fall on the ground and kill our young ones.'

The elephant guffawed arrogantly. He continued to shake the branches of the banyan tree. One by one, the nests fell on the ground. The eggs broke. A few young sparrows died due to the fall. The elephant seemed least bothered. After breaking a few branches, he proceeded towards his resting place. The older sparrows were aghast to see this. They began to weep inconsolably.

One of the sparrows said angrily, 'The elephant is so cruel and insensitive. Within a few minutes, he has destroyed our family.'

Another sparrow replied, 'The elephant is a big bully. He wants to use his power on small and weak creatures like us.'

A third sparrow said, 'We may be small but we are definitely not weak. We should teach him a lesson.'

All the sparrows got together in a huddle and discussed their plan of action. After coming up with a plan, they invited a bee, a woodpecker and a frog in their discussion and shared their thoughts. The guests were sympathetic towards the sparrows and were eager to help them out. They agreed to the plan.

The next morning, the bee approached the elephant and began to buzz near his ears. Hearing the continuous drone of the bee, the elephant closed its eyes. At that moment, the woodpecker, with his powerful beak, poked him in his eyes. The elephant began to panic and ran helter-skelter. Blinded, he was unable to figure out where he was going. Soon, he reached the edge of a steep valley. The frog stood nearby and began to croak loudly. On hearing the frog, the elephant assumed that he was near a river and leapt forward. He fell into the valley and died.

There are multiple lessons that one can learn from this anecdote. It teaches us humility and empathy. The elephant, overconfident because of his huge size, had no qualms about destroying the smaller creatures of the forest. However, those very small creatures gained victory in the end whereas he met a gory death. In the corporate world, too, we come across such elephants—intoxicated by power and money. They do not hesitate before crushing their subordinates. However, they should realize that the tables can easily turn.

Many times, when the subordinates obey their arrogant boss, it may not be a sign of respect but just plain fear. The moment the boss loses his post, his subordinates desert him.

The anecdote also shows the power of teamwork. A bee, a woodpecker and a frog got together and, with impeccable teamwork, were able to humble a huge elephant. Though none of these creatures individually was a match for the elephant, their combined synergy could overpower the giant. This story teaches us that small but sustained efforts can help us achieve even a Herculean task.

The Mousetrap

*The whole problem with the world is that fools and
fanatics are always so certain of themselves,
and wiser people so full of doubts.*

—Bertrand Russell

There lived a wise mouse in a farmer's home. Once, he observed the farmer holding a device in his hand and explaining to his wife, 'This is the latest mousetrap that I purchased from the city. It is so small in size that a mouse will not even notice it in the darkness.'

The mouse was stunned. A mousetrap—so small that he would not even know where it was kept—waiting to pounce on him and trap him! He got worried. He did not know what to do. In his anxiety, he began to run helter-skelter around the house.

He shouted, 'There is a mousetrap in the house! There is a mousetrap in the house! We are all doomed!'

Hearing his screams, the chicken replied nonchalantly, 'A mousetrap is of no consequence to me.'

Shocked at the chicken's reply, the mouse ran to a pig next and shouted, 'There is a mousetrap in the house! We will all get killed soon.'

The pig laughed, 'Why should I worry about a mousetrap? I am a pig, not a mouse!'

Next, the mouse ran to a cow and narrated his woes. The cow said, 'A mousetrap in the house? Go and hide yourself.'

The mouse asked the cow, 'Are you not worried about it?'

The cow laughed, 'Don't you see my huge body? Can I

ever get caught in a puny mousetrap?'

The mouse was dejected. It decided not to sleep inside the house. Instead, it spent the night outside in the field. The farmer kept the mousetrap in the kitchen since the mouse frequently hunted there for food. A few hours into the night, the farmer's wife heard a sound from the kitchen.

'Are there thieves in our house?' she asked her husband.

Her husband laughed, 'A mouse must have fallen into my new mousetrap.'

The wife was not satisfied with his reply. She decided to explore the kitchen. In the darkness, she had not noticed that a poisonous snake was trapped by the mousetrap. As she approached the mousetrap, the snake bit her. She screamed in agony and fell down. The farmer heard his wife's screams and came running to the kitchen. By then, she was lying unconscious on the floor. He immediately took her to a hospital in the nearby town.

The doctor advised the farmer to serve her hot chicken soup. The farmer returned to his farm. He killed the chicken and fed the soup to his wife. But the venom in his wife's body was taking its toll. The fever had not subsided. Her internal organs were getting damaged. Many of her relatives came to visit her. The farmer had to kill the pig to feed her relatives. A week later, the farmer's wife died. More relatives poured in for the funeral. Now the farmer had no choice but to kill his cow and serve its meat to the guests.

The mouse watched the chicken, the pig and the cow being slaughtered before his own eyes. He felt sad to lose his friends like this. If only they had heeded to his warning, they would have been alive.

Isn't this something that happens in real life too? Many times, we hear people complaining of their problems. Our immediate reaction is, 'Oh! It does not concern me. Why should I be bothered?' Instead, we should understand that when one person is facing a misfortune, we all are at risk. We must make an extra effort to understand each other's problems and look for solutions. Remember, another man's problem today can become your problem tomorrow.

A few years ago, my uncle used to stay in Jayanagar, an upmarket residential area of Bengaluru . During the initial years of his stay, Jayanagar was a quiet and calm nondescript area. It was considered the southern tip of Bengaluru and many local people used to even avoid visiting this suburb. However, one fine day, the state government decided to construct a huge shopping complex there—the biggest in the town. This project completely changed the topography and the face of Jayanagar. Soon, many shops, schools, colleges and houses were constructed near the complex. This locality became one of the most sought-after residential areas of the city. Land rates skyrocketed by around fifty times.

However, as all developments come with a price tag, so did this one. Traffic increased manifold, and as a result, roads began to witness more frequent and congested jams, especially near the shopping complex. The government had no choice but to widen the roads. In the process, many houses facing the main road were disturbed. The government purchased these houses at a paltry sum and began to demolish them further to widen the roads.

My uncle was among the people affected by this. Along with other families, he argued with the government officials that by broadening the roads and building flyovers, Jayanagar would turn into a concrete jungle and lose its charm of being one of the most green and serene areas of Bengaluru. They explained that it would not only lose its greenery but would also be affected adversely due to increase in traffic, noise and pollution. However, the government officials were unrelenting. They retorted that they could not hold back the city's development plans just because of the whims and fancies of a few residents.

For the next few weeks, my uncle and the affected residents tried their best to garner support from the other residents of Jayanagar. The affected residents were not only interested in retaining their houses but they also wanted to preserve the unique charm of the southern suburb. Unfortunately, they did not get any support from the other residents.

'We are not impacted by the widening of one road, so why are you bothering us?' was their irritated reply.

My uncle, being a civil engineer, was able to predict the future. He tried to reason with others, 'Today the government is widening our road, and only around twenty of us are affected. Tomorrow they might widen another fifteen roads and then hundreds of families will be affected.'

Unfortunately, the myopic residents of Jayanagar could not visualize the future. They remained silent spectators. A few weeks later, my uncle and twenty other families had to vacate their houses. Since they got very small amounts from the government, they could not afford to build another house in an upmarket area. Most of them moved to faraway suburbs.

A few years later, as the IT revolution bombarded Bengaluru, the population grew manifold. Not only Jayanagar but other adjoining residential areas too were adversely affected. Huge residential plots made way to commercial buildings and shopping malls. Traffic grew a hundredfold. The state government had no choice but to widen most roads in the suburbs. Thousands of families were affected. Just as it had happened to my uncle, these people, too, were given paltry amounts and were asked to move.

The biggest lesson from this real-life incident is that the problem of your friend or colleague or neighbour today can become your problem tomorrow. The best way to address the problem is to examine its long-term repercussions and immediately nip it in the bud rather than waiting for a small problem to snowball into a much bigger one.

Eyes Don't Always See It All

*It is as hard for the good to suspect evil,
as it is for the bad to suspect good.*

—Marcus Tullius Cicero

Once, two ascetics were passing through a village. The sun had set and the night was fast approaching. Hence, the duo decided to spend the night in the village. They knocked at the door of the first house they came across. It turned out to be the residence of a wealthy farmer. Though the farmer was wealthy, he was rude and arrogant. He was selfish and never liked helping others. As he opened the door, he noticed two tired-looking strangers in front of him.

'What do you want? If you are looking for food, my kitchen is empty,' the farmer growled and began to shut the door.

'Wait,' said the older ascetic, 'we are not looking for food.'

The farmer asked, 'Then? What do you seek in the middle of the night?'

'We are strangers in this village. It is quite dark outside. We felt it safer to spend the night in the village and proceed to our destination in the morning,' the ascetic explained.

The farmer was not keen on having two strangers sleeping in his house.

'I am a very poor farmer. I have no rooms to spare,' he lied.

'We can sleep in your stable,' replied the older ascetic.

'Are you sure?' the farmer asked. No one had ever slept in the smelly, dusty stable.

The ascetic smiled, 'Don't worry, sir, just show us the way!'

The farmer led the two ascetics to the stable. It was very

small and was stinking. The presence of two horses made the room appear even smaller and more cramped. The ascetics thanked the rich farmer for giving them sufficient space to sleep. The floor of the stable was bare and cold. Both the ascetics could hardly sleep that night. As the first rays of the sun hit the stable windows, the older ascetic sprang to his feet.

'Time for us to leave,' he told the younger ascetic.

As they passed the exit of the stable, the older ascetic saw a hole in the floor. Waving his divine wand, he repaired it. The younger ascetic asked him the reason behind this action, but the older one just smiled and remained silent. The next evening, the two ascetics passed another village. Once again, they decided to spend the night there.

The older ascetic suggested, 'As we did last night, we will halt in the first house that we come across.'

The younger ascetic nodded his head. A few minutes later, they arrived at an old and dilapidated farmhouse. They rang the doorbell and waited. For a long time, no one opened the door. Just as the ascetics were about to leave, they heard the front door open. An old farmer stood at the door.

'I am sorry it took a long time to open. Both my wife and I are suffering from arthritis. It takes a while to walk even five metres,' he apologized.

The farmer and his wife were old and poor. They had no one to help them. However, they had abundant hospitality. They treated the ascetics with whatever food they had. When it was time to sleep, the older ascetic suggested, 'Please show us your stable or cowshed. We will sleep there.'

The poor farmer was shocked. 'Oh no! How can I do that? You are our honoured guests. Though my house is small, you are welcome here. We all will sleep in the same room.'

The ascetics slept near the entrance of the room while the

farmer and his wife slept at the other end of the room.

Next morning, when the ascetics woke up, they heard the farmer crying. His pig, which he had looked after since the past four years had mysteriously died.

'He was so healthy. I wonder why he died so suddenly,' the farmer's wife wailed.

The two ascetics conveyed their heartfelt condolences and left the house. The younger ascetic was angry and disturbed. He glared at his older companion a couple of times but the latter pretended not to notice him. Only the occasional sound of a chirping bird broke the silence between them. Finally, the older ascetic turned towards the younger one and asked, 'Is something troubling you, my child?'

The younger ascetic glared, 'Troubling me? I am seething with anger!'

The older ascetic raised his eyebrows questioningly.

The younger one spoke, 'I just can't figure you out! The first farmer was so rude and arrogant. He was rich enough to afford food and room for us and yet he didn't offer us anything. We slept in a stinking stable. But you helped him by repairing a hole in the stable. The second farmer and his wife were so friendly, gentle and hospitable. They even gave up their food and beds. But what did they get? A dead pig.'

The older ascetic smiled, 'Oh young one! Don't just believe what your eyes see.'

Looking at the puzzled young ascetic, the older one explained, 'I agree that the first farmer was arrogant and selfish. I noticed a hole in his stable that, if explored, would have led to undiscovered hidden treasures. I fixed the hole so that the rude farmer would never find the hidden wealth.'

The younger one was not completely satisfied. 'What about the poor farmer? Why a dead pig?'

'Oh that! Well, if you recollect, both of us slept at the entrance of the farmer's room. While we were all sleeping, I noticed Lord Yama, the God of Death, walk in. I asked Him what had brought Him to the farmer's home. Lord Yama replied that He had come to take away the life of the farmer's wife. I begged him not to. He was adamant since her time was up. Finally, I negotiated with Him and convinced Him to take the pig instead. So, my dear son, don't always believe what you see.'

Doesn't this happen to us in our daily lives? When we experience or notice certain incidents in life, rarely do we look deep inside and interpret the purpose. We base our inferences on whatever we see in a superficial manner.

A small boy studying in kindergarten got the shock of his life. He had wet his shorts and the class was going to start in the next ten minutes. He had no clue how this had happened and didn't know what to do about it.

The light colour of the shorts made it worse for him. It made things obvious to anyone who cared to look at it. The boy was in tears. He knew that very soon, other boys would make fun of him and he would be the proverbial talk of the town.

He had no time to go home and change. Neither did he look ill enough to go and sleep in the infirmary. The only thought on his mind was, 'How do I run away from here?'

The boy began to pray desperately, 'Oh God! Please come to my rescue immediately. Please help me.'

A few minutes passed by. He was alarmed when he noticed his teacher walking in the corridor.

'Gosh! She will discover that I am standing here and will

laugh at me! So will my classmates,' he thought bitterly.

And then, it all happened in a flash. One of the girls, carrying a bottle of water, fell on him. Before he could realize what had happened, the bottle's cap had opened and its entire contents had fallen on his clothes. The girl gave a loud cry as the boy fell on the floor. The teacher and other students in the class rushed towards him. All of them began sympathizing with him.

The girl looked embarrassed. She offered to help but her teacher rebuked her, 'Go away! You have created enough mess already!'

All the other students laughed at her. Initially, the boy was very upset with the girl.

'How reckless is she! How dare she spill water on me? My clothes are all wet!' the boy thought angrily.

However, a few minutes later, he realized that the girl's accidental fall had proved to be a blessing in disguise. Since his shorts and shirt were completely drenched in water, no one could notice that he had wet his shorts. The girl had actually saved him! The teacher asked him to go to the gymnasium and borrow a spare pair of shorts. Later, in the evening, the boy met the girl and said, 'I don't know how to thank you for what happened this afternoon.'

The girl smiled. 'I, too, wet my shorts once,' she said.

We should realize that not everyone who seems to be harming us is our enemy. The opposite is also true—not everyone who appears to be helping us is our friend.

Poor Little Rich Man

*There is a gigantic difference between
earning a great deal of money and being rich.*

—Marlene Dietrich

A rich man's son wanted to understand the meaning of poverty. He asked his father to explain.

His father said, 'A picture is worth a thousand words. Let me show you what poverty means.'

The following weekend, the father took his son to his ancestral village. He was determined to show the tough life of the villagers and later compare it with their own comfortable lifestyle.

'My son will be more grateful to me for all that I have done for him after he sees how people in villages live,' thought the father as their car sped across the dusty roads of the country.

As soon as they reached the village, his father drove straight to their ancestral home. It was huge but ill-equipped—with just the bare necessities. As they entered the dilapidated building, the father showed his son his bedroom. Instead of air-conditioners, it had open-air ventilators. Unlike the distempered walls in their home, these walls were plastered with dried cow dung. The father could see his son grimace.

A few hours later, they sat down for lunch. The humble and meal consisted of dry rotis and sabzi. A steel tumbler containing lassi marked the end of a simple meal. After lunch, the father took his son for a stroll in the village. They passed lakes, meadows and hillocks as they walked towards the market. Petty shops were lined up on both sides of the dusty, narrow street. There were no shopping centres and malls. Bullock carts and horse carriages replaced Mercedes and BMWs. The next couple of days, the father and son explored the entire village. They talked to various villagers. On Sunday evening, it was time to depart. On the drive back to the city, the father asked his son, 'How was your experience, my son?'

The son immediately replied, 'It was great, Daddy!'

The father was sure that he had heard it wrong. He repeated his question.

His son replied, 'Thanks for showing me poverty, Daddy.'

The father smiled, 'Elaborate, my son. What did you learn during your stay?'

His son explained, 'We have just one dog whereas each farmer had more than ten cows and buffaloes. We have a small swimming pool and they have a huge lake. We can see the sky only from the balcony of our house, whereas they sleep daily in the open where they can see the entire horizon. We buy stale canned food from supermarkets whereas they grow their own vegetables and cook it fresh. We protect our homes with barbed wires and fences. They guard their homes with trust and faith.'

Hearing this, the boy's father was stunned.

The boy smiled, 'Thanks a lot for showing me how poor we are. I have now fully understood the meaning of poverty.'

Like most of us, the rich man had assumed that wealth was directly proportional to happiness. He wanted to boast about his lavish lifestyle and compare it with that of the poor villagers. However, he received a rude shock when he heard his wise son.

Who says wisdom comes with age?

A few years ago, I used to work for a Swiss multinational

company. My office was located in Whitefield, a faraway suburb in Bengaluru. It used to take me a couple of hours to commute each way. Since Whitefield has numerous IT companies, the traffic mainly consists of IT professionals driving down to work. It is a common sight to see couples travelling together to their place of work. Since Whitefield is also one of the fastest growing suburbs in the city, one can see construction happening everywhere. Many trucks carrying construction materials can be seen plying on the roads. Construction workers and labourers are packed like sardines inside these trucks. They do not even have a proper place to sit. A majority of them have to keep standing throughout the long journey.

You would expect the rich IT couples to be relaxed, contented and happy, having achieved a high standard of living and enjoying all the materialistic comforts. You would also expect the construction workers to sit in the cramped trucks with woebegone faces, probably cursing their ill-fate.

However, the reality is generally the opposite!

I have observed rich IT couples sitting with mournful looks on their faces—as if they do not know from where their next meal will come! In some cases, the husband is on a teleconference and the wife is twiddling with her smartphone or eating her hastily cooked breakfast. Not a single muscle on their face exudes joy. I often ponder over their worried looks and wonder what calamity has fallen on them to make them look so dejected and troubled.

On the other hand, the construction workers in the truck look far more cheerful. Despite not being able to afford one square meal a day, their faces are filled with contentment as they merrily chat with each other. Their sparkling eyes, cheerful laughter and friendly patting on each other's backs is a joy to behold.

This was a lesson to me. I discovered that there was very little correlation between materialistic comforts and happiness. Though money plays an important role in leading a comfortable life, it does not always ensure happiness. The factors that decide a person's contentment are quite different from worldly comforts.

No Pain, No Gain

*A rebirth out of spiritual adversity causes us
to become new creatures.*

—James E. Faust

Once, a man sitting in a park saw the cocoon of a butterfly. He noticed that the cocoon had a very small opening and a butterfly was trying to come out of it. Curious, the man decided to observe it. Many minutes later, the butterfly was still struggling to come out of the small hole in the cocoon.

The man was kind-hearted and wanted to help the butterfly. After a while, he was unable to watch the struggle of the poor creature anymore. He grabbed a pair of scissors and cut the cocoon into two. The butterfly was then able to come out easily.

He noticed that the butterfly that emerged had a swollen body and underdeveloped wings. He did not pay much attention to it since it was still very young. 'Hopefully, within a day or two, it will become a full-fledged butterfly and fly away.'

He left the park with these thoughts in his mind. When he woke up the next morning, he remembered the butterfly in the park.

'Let me go and see if it has flown away,' he thought to himself.

He dressed hastily and went to the same spot in the park. He didn't expect to find the creature there since butterflies are never known to remain in one place. Imagine his surprise when he noticed the butterfly still crawling in the same place! Its body was still swollen and its wings remained small and shrivelled.

'Maybe I am being too hasty! It may take some time to develop. Let me come back tomorrow,' he thought and returned home.

A couple of days later, he came back to the park. He was shocked to find that the butterfly still had a swollen body and was struggling to walk. Its wings remained underdeveloped.

For the rest of its life, the butterfly was unable to fly.

Though the man had a good soul, he did not understand God's intentions. God wanted the butterfly to struggle its way through the cocoon so that it would not only get rid of its bodily fluid but also strengthen its wings. By breaking the cocoon, the man had made it very easy for the butterfly to come out of its cocoon. It neither lost its fluid nor could it toughen its wings.

Sometimes, in our lives, too, we need struggles to strengthen us. If God allowed us to lead an easy life devoid of obstacles, wouldn't we get crippled like the butterfly?

During my childhood, I remember watching one of the early films depicting the Shaolin martial arts—primarily kung fu. In the film, a young student flees to the Shaolin Temple to learn kung fu and take revenge from those who had tried to kill him. A major part of the story is about the gruelling training that he has to undergo. At times, his teacher seems ruthless, almost evil. However, as we watch the young lad master the art of kung fu and go on to become one of the best kung fu masters in the kingdom, we realize that the teacher had the burning desire to see his student succeed. His seemingly heartless behaviour was to prepare his student for the future.

My sons often complain about certain teachers at the school being extremely strict and demanding. The homework and assignments keep them awake until midnight. No wonder they view their teachers as their enemies!

I tell my sons that the initial formative years of their lives are going to shape their future. The amount of hard work and effort they put in their childhood is going to have a huge impact on the quality of the rest of their lives. I counsel them to look at their teachers as their mentors, guides and well-wishers, who are concerned about their future. The plethora of tasks and assignments given to them is to 'make' them and not 'break' them.

Nail It!

You will not be punished for your anger,
you will be punished by your anger.

—Buddha

Once, there lived a boy who was the only child of his parents. Though the boy was bright and talented, he was very rude and arrogant. His bad temper led to frequent fights with his classmates and the other boys living in the neighbourhood. He had absolutely no respect for his teachers and parents.

His parents were concerned about his boorish behaviour. Though his mother often scolded him, it had no impact on the boy. One day, his father had an idea. He took his son to their garage and showed him a wooden log.

The father instructed his son, 'Each time you get upset with someone, don't shout at that person. Instead, come here and hammer a nail into the wooden log.'

The boy agreed to follow his father's instructions. During the rest of the day, the boy lost his temper on four occasions. Later that night, the boy went to the garage to hammer the nails. However, the boy found the wooden log very tough. Despite having a good hammer and sharp nails, he struggled to hammer the nails into the log of wood.

At the end of the first week, the boy had hammered around forty nails into the wooden log. He found this very tiring. The boy realized that controlling his temper was simpler than hammering nails into the wooden log!

Slowly, the boy began to make attempts to control his

temper. The following week, he lost his temper only on twenty occasions. In the third week, it was just ten. A few weeks later, he did not lose his temper at all. The boy was proud of his accomplishment. He told his parents about it. His father took him to the garage once again and showed him the nail-ridden wooden log.

He told his son, 'Each day that you don't lose your temper even once, you get to remove one nail.'

For the next few days, the boy controlled his temper. Every night, he would remove a nail from the wooden log. After a few weeks, the boy proudly told his father that all the nails had been removed.

His father said, 'Can you show me the wooden log?'

The son took him to the garage.

The father pointed to the log and said, 'Look, son! You have managed to remove all the nails but have you noticed the condition of the log? Do you see the holes that are left? From now on, the wooden log will remain with these holes and scars, no matter what you do.'

There are numerous occasions when we lose our temper, only to regret it later. However, we do not notice the scars such instances cause. Even after many years, the wounds remain—like the holes on the wooden log.

My second book *Pitch It!* is a book about cricket and management. It draws analogies between the cricketing and corporate world and drives home several important management lessons. As it was a book on cricket and management, I thought it appropriate to invite one cricketing icon and one corporate honcho as chief guests for the book launch. I requested Syed Kirmani and T.V. Mohandas Pai to do the honours.

After the event, I requested both the chief guests to sign my book. I noticed Syed Kirmani scribbling a sentence before signing off. At that time, I did not pay much attention to what he had written. I assumed that it was the usual 'good luck' or 'best wishes' kind of message.

However, later that night, after I reached home, I opened the book and turned to the page that he had autographed. Syed Kirmani had written a famous quote that has remained etched in my mind until date—'It is nice to be important but more important to be nice!'

True, is it not? While we are busy working hard towards achieving success, fame, glory and importance in the society, we forget another equally (or more) important aspect in life—the aspect of being nice.

When I joined Motorola (one of the biggest MNCs in the world) in the 1990s, I was hoping to learn the latest in cutting-edge technology and become the best and most innovative engineer among my friends and peers. On my first day, after the initial joining formalities, I was asked to report for the formal corporate induction. There were around twenty-five of us in the conference room. The CEO of the organization gave us a warm and inspirational 'welcome speech' that charged us up.

At the end of his speech, he smiled and said, 'I am going to give each one of you a card—popularly known as the "Motorola card". I would like each one of you to carefully read what's written on it and remember it for the rest of your lives.'

I was expecting the card to contain details of the organization's structure or various addresses and contact numbers or financial figures. Imagine my surprise when I noticed that it only had two sentences:

1. Constant respect to people
2. Uncompromising integrity

These were the 'Motorola values' that had been with the company for many decades and would remain so. While there is a strong desire amongst us to be rich and famous, we need to also have the desire to remain nice and respect other people and their views, however diverse they may be.

In corporate life, you might have noticed many arrogant people getting immense respect from their team members and fellow colleagues. Have you ever wondered why? The answer is simple: what you are seeing is not a display of respect; in reality, it is a mix of fear and sycophancy. The power and status of that arrogant person evokes a timid and obsequious behaviour from his team members. Would the same people respect him if he retired or moved to a different organization? Probably not.

Treat everyone with kindness and respect—even those who are rude to you, not because they are nice, but because you are!

Santushti (Contentment)

Santushti or 'being satisfied with what we have' is the first step towards attaining happiness. Socrates rightly said, 'He who is not contented with what he has, would not be contented with what he would like to have.' No amount of comfort, riches or fame can give a dissatisfied person any happiness. The happiest people do not always have the best of everything; they just make the best of everything.

The Three Dolls

Wise men speak because they have something to say; fools because they have to say something.

—Anonymous

Once there lived a king in Rajasthan. As he was getting old, he decided to perform the coronation ceremony of his young prince. At the end of the ceremony, he was showered with expensive gifts from kings who had travelled from faraway places to attend this function. The prince received dozens of horses, camels and elephants. He was also gifted silk robes, silk turbans and the finest gold chains.

The prince noticed an old ascetic standing near the doorway of the court. He walked to the holy man, bowed before him, and said, 'Oh holy one, it is very kind of you to attend my function. Please bless me.'

The old ascetic blessed him and said, 'I would like to give you a gift.'

The prince replied, 'Swamiji, you've blessed me and that is my biggest gift.'

The ascetic smiled and opened his cloth bag. He pulled out three dolls and handed them over to the prince.

The prince laughed, 'Swamiji, I am a Kshatriya! My job is to fight against my enemies and protect my subjects. What will I do with these dolls?'

The ascetic smiled once again and explained, 'These are no ordinary dolls, my child. Let me show you something.'

Saying this, the holy man handed over some pieces of thread to the young prince and said, 'Please hold the first doll in your hand and pass a thread through its ear. Tell me what happens when you do that.'

The prince did as he was told. The thread went in through one ear and came out through the other.

The ascetic explained, 'These are the kind of people who don't retain anything in their mind. There is no use telling them anything. Now do the same with the second doll.'

The prince passed the thread through the ear of the second doll. The thread came out of its mouth.

'These are the people who can't keep any secrets. Tell them anything and they will tell the whole world about it,' explained the ascetic.

Now, the prince passed the thread through the ear of the third doll, but it did not come out. He was puzzled and he asked the ascetic for an explanation.

'These are the people who take in information, but they never let anything out,' the ascetic replied.

With folded hands, the prince asked, 'Oh, wise one! Please tell me which kind of person should one aspire to be?'

The ascetic put his hand into his cloth bag and pulled out another doll. He then asked him to put the same thread thrice into the doll's ear. The first time when the prince put the thread into its ear, it came out of the other ear. The second time, it came out of its mouth, and the third time it did not come out at all.

'What does this mean?' the prince asked.

The ascetic explained, 'One should aspire to be someone who knows when not to listen, when to speak and when to remain silent.'

The prince bowed before the ascetic and thanked him for his invaluable advice.

❖

The fourth doll is the right combination of the first three dolls. It is very important that we, too, follow the same principles as the fourth doll.

When we hear any kind of gossip, however interesting it may sound, we should behave like the first doll—not listen and pay attention to it. When we hear any information that is useful to others, we should act like the second doll—spread the knowledge for the benefit of others. There is a general reluctance to spreading knowledge among others because we equate 'knowledge' with 'power'. However, it is important to understand that if you light a second candle with a lit candle, the light of the lit candle does not diminish.

There are instances where we may receive confidential information. These should not be revealed to anyone—that is when we need to behave like the third doll. Whether we hold some authority or are a commoner, there are numerous occasions when someone confides in you, and it is best to not reveal it to anyone.

Nip It the Socrates Way

*Gossip is when you hear something
you like about someone you don't.*

—Earl Wilson

Socrates was one of the greatest philosophers in the world, well-known for his wisdom. His philosophical views and teachings are legendary and relevant even today.

One day, one of his friends asked him, 'Do you know what I just heard…'

Socrates interrupted him, 'Hang on! Before you proceed, I would like to ask you three questions. If you pass my test, then you may proceed with what you want to say.'

His friend agreed and asked him to conduct the three-questions test.

The great philosopher asked, 'The first question is known as the "truth" test. Are you absolutely certain that whatever you plan to tell me is the truth?'

His friend hesitatingly replied, 'Well, I…err…I cannot say for sure that it is the truth. I just heard it from my friend, who heard it from his friend, and he…'

Socrates once again interrupted him, 'Stop! You have failed the "truth" test. You do not know if what you are going to say is true or not.'

His friend asked him, 'What is your second question?'

Socrates replied, 'My second test is known as "goodness" test. Whatever you plan to tell me—is it something which is good to hear?'

His friend shook his head and replied, 'No, in fact, it is neither good nor pleasant to hear.'

Socrates frowned, 'Well, you have failed the second test too. It is neither true nor good. I hope you fare better in the third test.'

Disheartened, his friend asked, 'What is the third question?'

Socrates smiled and replied, 'The third question refers to "usefulness". So, what you are about to tell me, will it be of any use to me?'

His friend once again shook his head. 'It is not at all useful,' he replied meekly.

Socrates exclaimed, 'You have failed the third test too! What you wanted to tell me is neither true, nor good, nor useful. It is plain gossip. I consider it a waste of time to listen to your gossip.'

Saying this, the great philosopher got up and walked away.

Don't we experience this frequently in our professional as well as personal lives? Very often, our colleagues come to us to share 'juicy gossips' about a fellow worker in the office. What is our normal reaction to such behaviour? I am sure that in most cases we not only give a patient hearing to what they are saying, but we also end up adding our own masala to it!

I completely agree with the famous adage: 'An idle mind is a devil's workshop'. The amount of gossip that happens in an organization is inversely proportional to the workload. I have worked in organizations where the workload was so high that we did not even have time to breathe, forget gossip!

The same is true in our personal lives as well. The amount of gossip that takes place within a family is huge; it is probably worse in a joint family, since there are more 'family members' (read 'opportunities') for gossip!

A woman with a modern outlook often becomes a soft target in a conservative family setup. Similarly, a young man with bold views is viewed as an aberration. These kinds of people are generally easy meat for malicious gossip. I personally believe in giving every individual the benefit of doubt. When anyone comes to me with a juicy titbit about another person, my first reaction is: 'How do you know it is the truth?' When people pass judgements based on one side of the story, my natural response is to ask them, 'Have you heard both sides of the story?'

In most cases, the response that I receive, with a shake of the head, is: 'I am not sure if that it is the truth; but everyone is talking about it.' Just because 'everyone is talking about it, does it become true?

The second question that Socrates asked was: 'Whatever you plan to tell me, is it something which is good to hear?' It is a well-known fact that bad news travels faster than good news. Similarly, people love to share anecdotes that put other people in poor light. You may do ninety-nine out of 100 tasks very well but your colleagues and relatives will talk only about the one that did not go well! Socrates knew about this too well and that was why he was quite sure that what he was going to hear would be nothing good.

The third question that Socrates asked was about the usefulness of the information. This was linked to the first question about truthfulness. If a statement is not true, the chances of it being useful are almost nil. After all, why would a false piece of information be useful?

So, the next time someone approaches you to divulge any information, please ask them these 'three questions'.

The Muddled Mind

*If you correct your mind,
the rest of your life will fall into place.*

—Lao Tzu

One day, Gautama Buddha was crossing a forest with his followers. The scorching afternoon sun had tired them out. Seeing the weariness of his followers, Lord Buddha suggested resting under the shade of a banyan tree. His followers readily agreed.

A few minutes later, one of the disciples asked Buddha, 'O Learned One! My mind is often consumed by worries and stress. I am constantly disturbed. Please advise me how to overcome it.'

Lord Buddha just smiled at him and said nothing.

A few minutes later, Buddha felt thirsty. He asked one of his disciples to get him water. His follower went in search of water and came across a lake. As he was about to dip his pot into the water, he noticed some villagers washing their clothes and utensils in the lake. As a result, the water was muddy.

The disciple thought, 'How can I give dirty water to Lord Buddha?'

Thinking thus, he returned to the banyan tree.

Buddha asked his disciple, 'Why have you returned with an empty pot?'

His disciple replied, 'O Holy One! The water I found was muddy, so I did not get it for you. I will go to the lake again and check if the water is cleaner in some time.'

Buddha just smiled at him and said nothing.

After a few minutes, the disciple returned to the lake. He was relieved to see that the villagers had left the scene. As he was about to dip his pot into the lake, he noticed a few cows stepping into the lake. The water once again became muddy. Disappointed, the disciple went back to Lord Buddha and said, 'I am sorry that I have not been able to fulfil your simple request.'

The Lord just smiled at him and said, 'Please go again after some time.'

A few minutes later, the disciple once went to the lake again. By then, the cows had left. He noticed that the mud had settled down and the water was now crystal clear. He collected the water and went back to Lord Buddha.

Lord Buddha asked his disciple, 'What did you learn from this episode?'

His disciple looked confused and had no answer to Buddha's query.

Lord Buddha asked, 'Why did you visit the lake thrice?'

His disciple replied, 'The first couple of visits to the lake were in vain because the water was muddy. I had to return empty-handed each time.'

Lord Buddha asked, 'How did you make sure that it was clear the third time?'

'I just waited for a while. I allowed the mud to settle down.'

The Lord smiled and said, 'The same is the case with your mind. It is often disturbed, just like the lake. When the lake water turns muddy, you should not disturb it further. Leaving it untouched automatically allows the mud to settle down and makes the water clean. Likewise, when you are in a confused or angry state, just allow things to settle down. It will become right.'

In rural parts of India, it is quite common to see villagers stepping into lakes for daily chores. They use lakes to collect water, bathe and wash clothes. The farmers even wash their cattle and villagers clean their utensils in the water of the lake. All these activities disturb the equilibrium of the water. It causes the mud at the bottom to rise to the top. Each time a human or an animal steps into a lake, the water becomes muddy. However, once the intruder leaves the lake, the mud once again settles at the bottom and the water becomes still.

Our minds, too, are similar to these lakes. Under normal circumstances, our mind is calm and composed. However, thoughts of greed, envy, hatred and lust are likely to make our mind agitated, angry, disappointed and spiteful. These thoughts and feelings are similar to the villagers and their cattle. The more the villagers and cattle, the more turbulence there is. The longer they stay and disrupt the water, the longer it takes the mud to settle down. This is true with our minds too—more negative thoughts mean more turbulence. The longer these negative thoughts linger in our minds, the longer it takes to return to normalcy. In both cases, the normal state returns only when the invaders have left it.

If you want your mind to remain calm, serene and pure, then free yourselves from such invaders and allow your mind to settle down.

How Heavy is Your Glass?

*Our fatigue is often caused not by work,
but by worry, frustration and resentment*

—Dale Carnegie

A teacher brought an empty glass and a bottle of water in the class. He poured water into the glass, held it up, and asked his students, 'What do you see in my hand?'

The students shouted in unison, 'A glass of water!'

The teacher asked, 'How much does it weigh?'

The answers varied—100 grams, 200 grams, 400 grams, and even one kilogram! The teacher asked a few students to come in turns and hold the glass in their hands. To each of them, he asked the same question, 'Is it easy or difficult to hold this glass of water?'

Each student gave the same answer, 'Very easy!'

The teacher smiled and said, 'Now, if I ask you to hold the same glass of water for thirty minutes, how would you feel?'

The answer varied from 'bit difficult' to 'difficult' to 'quite difficult'.

The teacher asked, 'If you have to hold it for two hours?'

All the students replied, 'Very difficult, sir!'

'If you had to hold it for a day?' the teacher queried.

'Our arm would ache severely. We might even have to visit the doctor,' was the response.

The teacher pretended to be shocked and asked, 'Why is it very difficult? After all, neither the glass nor the water has changed.'

One of the students replied, 'Sir, holding the glass of water for a long time will cause stress to our muscles. Hence, the severe pain.'

The teacher replied, 'Very good! Now tell me, how do I get rid of the pain?'

Another student promptly responded, 'Keep the glass on the table and rest your hand for some time.'

The teacher replied, 'Excellent! Life's problems are also similar. If you keep them in your head for a short time, you can tolerate them. If you keep them for a longer duration, then your head begins to hurt. If you keep them for an unusually long time, then you can be hospitalized.'

One of the students asked, 'So, what do we do?'

The teacher replied, 'Just like the arm stops aching once you put the glass down on the table, you need to put your problems to rest every night. When you go to sleep, your mind should be clear and free from all problems. This will help you wake up fresh the next morning.'

Many of life's problems start in a small way and they are light in nature—like the glass of water. However, when you hold on to to the problem for a long time, it becomes like the glass of water in your hand. It grows heavier with each passing minute. We keep the glass on the nearest table to free our arms from that exercise. This is done to rest our hand and avoid unnecessary strain on our muscles. So what prevents us from doing the same with our problems?

Today, two of the major illnesses in India are high blood pressure and diabetes. While it is a known fact that our genes, sedentary lifestyle and food habits are some of the common causes, it would also be good to know about the stress levels that cause these dreaded diseases.

Half a century ago, we used to earn a low salary, but we probably had a much higher happiness quotient. Our wants and needs were fewer. Most Indians struggled to acquire basic necessities in life. Having an air-conditioner or a TV in the 1990s was considered a luxury. However, back then, people seemed to be happy and content with whatever they had.

Over the years, our needs changed. Initially, the changes were gradual. However, during the past couple of years, thanks to the IT boom, the changes in our lifestyles have been more rapid. While more and more families are able to afford expensive electronic gadgets, consumer durables and holidays in exotic locations abroad, it comes with a price—the price of stress.

In a jet-set era where competition is high and the products' shelf lives are shrinking, it is imperative to deliver fast. In a rush to shorten 'time to market', the entire chain of product design, manufacture, sales and customer support is under tremendous pressure. This translates into stress. Sophisticated communication devices have aggravated the situation. During the olden times, a person would leave behind his office problems at 5 p.m. on a Friday evening. His next thoughts of his official tasks would come only on Monday morning in the office.

However, this is no longer true. Once laptops were invented, everyone was expected to periodically log into the office server from home and respond to important mails. This led to concepts like 'working on weekends' and 'working from home'. The only 'quality time' that an employee had was when he was not logged into his system.

Unfortunately, with the advent of smartphones, things have become even worse. With the smartphones being connected to data networks, who needs a laptop to log into a server? Your emails are arriving in the 'inbox' every minute of your life! The expectations from the employers, too, have gone high—'I have provided you with a mobile phone not to play Pokémon GO, but to attend to important phone calls and messages.'

In such a fast-paced world, where we carry our problems in our pockets, it is imperative to dedicate quality time for yourself and your family. Otherwise, it will be a case of constantly carrying the glass of water in your hand and unnecessarily stressing yourself. The choice is yours!

Present is a Gift

*It is not how much we have, but
how much we enjoy, that makes happiness.*

—Charles Spurgeon

It was a hot and humid afternoon in Goa. Most tourists were cooling themselves by taking a dip in the Arabian Sea. A fisherman had just finished his work for the day. Satisfied with his catch, he decided to take some rest. He managed to find a canopy for himself and began resting in its shade.

A rich American tourist passed by. He was shocked to see the young fisherman resting in the middle of the day.

He shook the fisherman gently and asked, 'Why are you not working? Why are you wasting your time?'

The fisherman replied, 'I have finished my work and I am now resting for the day.'

The American replied, 'Finished so soon? How many fish did you catch today?'

The fisherman replied, 'Around 150.'

The American laughed, 'Just 150! And you are satisfied?'

Seeing the puzzled look on the fisherman's face, the American continued, 'Young man! At your age, I used to work fifteen hours a day! If you work like me, you will catch more than a 1000 fish every day.'

The fisherman asked innocently, 'What will I achieve by catching so many fish?'

'Don't you understand? The more fish you catch, the more you will be able to sell. This will help you earn more money,' the tourist replied.

'What will I do with so much money?' the fisherman asked.

The American explained, 'Currently, you have small fishing boats. With more cash, you can buy bigger and better boats. You can try deep-sea fishing. Your catch will increase a hundredfold. You will become wealthier!'

'How will that help me?' the fisherman asked.

The American tourist was beginning to lose his patience. He replied, 'If you become wealthy, you can buy more boats and hire more fishermen. They will do all the fishing. You can become rich like me, and enjoy your life on the beach.'

The fisherman simply smiled and replied, 'Am I not doing that already?'

In today's fast-paced life, we are so busy minting money that we do not have any time to enjoy it. Right from the time children start school, they face stiff competition from their peers. It is hammered into their tiny heads that if they have to survive the rat race then they should constantly stay ahead of others. It is taught that the means are not important, what matters is the result. 'If you have to break a few rules, go ahead' is the advice given by their parents.

As children grow up, they are made aware of the significance of board examinations. The parents decide what academic course their children should take. They even dream of the institution their children will graduate from, and such parents try their best to ensure that their dreams are fulfilled.

In the bargain, the children are the ones who suffer. I have known many fathers whose aspiration was to graduate from the IITs, NITs and the IIMs, but unfortunately, they did not make it into any of these hallowed institutions. Their sole aim in life then became to ensure that their son or daughter graduated from one of these institutions. Such parents do not even try to find out if their child is interested in studying engineering or management, let alone evaluate their child's probability of getting selected in the entrance exams to these prestigious institutions.

Recently, I met an old friend after a long time. After exchanging the initial pleasantries, I asked him about his family. He proudly told me, 'I have one son who is studying in VII standard. I would like him to graduate from IIT Bombay or IIT Delhi.'

When I asked him the reason, he stated, 'I did not get a good JEE rank, so I did not get selected in any of the IITs. I would like my son to fulfil my dream.'

I asked him, 'Are you sure your son wants to study in one the IITs?'

He looked at me as if I had gone crazy, and was quick to respond, 'Who wouldn't!'

'How do you know your son wants to study engineering? Have you ever asked him?' I questioned him.

By now, my friend had concluded that I was indeed crazy. He retorted angrily, 'He is a bright student, and has always topped his class. What better course than engineering?'

'Why? Can't bright students become doctors, journalists or chartered accountants?' I asked him.

Have you ever investigated the 'IIT, NIT, IIM' syndrome? Why would most parents want their children to study in one of these premier institutes? Is it the teaching? Is it the infrastructure? Is it the content of the syllabus?

Sadly, in majority of the cases, none of the parents are even aware of the above attributes of a college. Their judgement is purely based on two factors—the brand image of the institution and the campus placement after graduation. The brand image of the institution is directly linked to peer pressure. Nothing gives more joy to a parent than to boast of their child's prestigious institution and its credentials. These days, it is a very common to see proud parents posting pictures of their children's convocation ceremony on Facebook, but only if the child has graduated from a premier institution! Have you ever wondered why most colleges periodically publish the campus placement data in leading newspapers, magazines and websites? Why this obsession with campus recruitment and placement?

In most cases, it is to advertise that the graduate will launch his professional career by joining one of the top companies in the country. If a parent is obsessed with IIT, NIT or IIM when the child is still a toddler, now the same parent is dreaming of a lucrative career as he watches his child grow into an adult. Why do parents want their children to work in top organizations? Is it the nature of the work or the content? Or is it the work environment?

In most cases, the parents are unaware of the above. The sole purpose of them wanting their children to join an esteemed company is to see them make more and more money. The key driver is neither job satisfaction nor work-life balance. It is always money! This is not to say that there are no cases of young professionals chucking their highly paid corporate jobs and joining an educational institute as professors at less than half the salary. But these are just a few exceptions.

The greed to earn more money continues. A few years after a person starts his professional career, he gets married. Naturally, his expenses increase. As his family grows, so do the expenses. The desire to own a car and a house becomes irresistible. Peer pressure again plays a major factor in influencing such desires. Though most professionals face a midlife crisis, very few of them throw their jobs away and do something that they are passionate about. They begin thinking about the expenses in their children's marriage. Then post-retirement blues also begin to haunt them.

Haven't you come across statements like:

'I wanted to teach underprivileged children, but never got an opportunity to do so.'

'I wanted to paint and draw, but did not have the time to pursue my passions.'

'I wanted to travel the world, but that never happened.'

Are these examples of lack of time or effort? No, these examples highlight man's obsession with money, which has become an overriding priority over all other activities.

This does not mean that we do not want to enjoy life; in fact, we definitely do. Unfortunately, we keep postponing such indulgences until it is too late. Finally, we either grow too old and weak to pursue our interests or die before we can follow our passions.

Priorities

*Efficiency is doing things right;
effectiveness is doing the right things.*

—Peter Drucker

Once upon a time, a professor asked his students to speak on time management and prioritization of tasks. None of them could give him a convincing answer. With a glass jar in his hands, the professor took the students to a nearby field. He dropped a couple of rocks in the jar and asked the students if the jar was full. The students said 'yes' in unison.

'Can I put more rocks in the bottle?' the professor asked.

All the students shook their heads. The professor then picked small pebbles lying on the ground and put them in the jar. He looked at the students, smiled and said, 'Wasn't I able to put more pebbles in the jar?'

The students nodded. The professor asked one of the students, 'What is the condition of the jar?'

The student replied promptly, 'It is full, sir.'

The professor bent down, picked up some sand, and poured it into the jar. The sand filled the remaining nooks and crannies.

'Is the jar full now? Can I add more sand into it?' he asked the students.

The students replied, 'No, sir, the jar is full.'

Next, he took a glass of water and poured it into the jar.

He asked the students, 'What did you learn from this experiment?'

One of the students replied, 'Each time we thought the

jar was filled to the brim, it wasn't.'

Another said, 'You could accommodate more items into the jar than we could think!'

The professor explained, 'Both of you are right. Do not get deceived by what you see initially. What else did you notice?'

One of the students replied, 'The sequence also makes a difference.'

The professor smiled and said, 'Excellent point! In life, we call it prioritization. Whatever you have observed here is applicable in your daily lives too.'

No one can deny that the pace of life has increased more than ten times during the past few decades. Right from young children to middle-aged people, everyone seems to be in a rush to do things. Whenever I see people jostling each other on the streets, or drivers breaking traffic rules, I wonder what these people do with the extra minute they gain. When you meet a long-lost friend at a social gathering and ask him, 'How are you? It has been long since you came home. Where have you been?', the answer is invariably, 'I have been very busy.'

Once I invited a friend to my home. When I asked him the same questions, the reason he gave was classic. He replied, 'You stay very far away from my home. Why don't you pay me a visit?'

For a minute, I blinked. I remembered what my geometry teacher had taught me in school, 'The distance between point A and B is same as the distance between point B and A.'

In the above anecdote, when the professor placed rocks in the jar, the students initially thought that there was no room for anything else. However, the professor cleverly accommodated the smaller pebbles in it. Once again, the students felt that there was no more space in the jar. Now, the professor added sand in the jar, followed by water. While a normal person would have just placed a few rocks inside the jar, the wise professor could fill rocks, pebbles, sand and water within the same space!

Rocks are the topmost priority due to their size, so they should be put first. Then come the pebbles, followed by sand, and finally, water. If you put sand in the very beginning, you will not have any space for pebbles. Similarly, if you put the smaller pebbles in the beginning, you won't be able to adjust the rocks. Remember, your sequence should be based on your priorities.

Similarly, we often believe that we have no time for our family and friends because of the frantic pace of our lives. However, the reality is quite different. The jar represents the time that each of us has. The rocks, pebbles, sand and water represent the various tasks in our lives. Our family and health is of prime importance. That is represented by the rocks. The pebbles are next in priority. That could be our job or source of income. Next is the sand, which can be a bit lower in priority, such as our house or car. The water comes in the end. This includes the activities that are not high on our priority list.

A common question that newspaper journalists, friends and relatives ask me is, 'You are an IT professional and the common belief is that the pace of life in your field is very fast and tough. How do you manage to write books? Where do you get the time to do it?'

I always smile and reply that it is a myth that only IT professionals are busy and leading high-pressure lives. In today's world, all jobs are equally busy and taxing. It is in our hands to prioritize our lives.

If you spend seventy hours a week on official work, then writing books is probably not your cup of tea. If you love watching movies, shopping, bowling and eating out every weekend, then you probably cannot dream of pursuing other hobbies. If you are serious about pursuing your passion, make it your number-one priority of life. It should be the 'rocks and pebbles' of your life, not the 'sand and water'.

Peace of Mind

*Life is pleasant. Death is peaceful.
It's the transition that's troublesome.*

—Isaac Asimov

There once lived an old farmer in a village, and he spent most of his time in his paddy fields. One day, he lost his watch in the field. He looked for it everywhere, but could not find it. This worried the farmer, as the watch was quite expensive. With a sad face, he walked towards his home. A few farmers passing him noticed his dejected face.

'What is the matter?' they asked.

The farmer replied, 'I lost my watch while working in the fields this afternoon! Unfortunately, I could not find it even after a thorough search.'

One of the farmers remarked, 'Take us to your field. We will search for it.'

The farmer replied, 'I will give a suitable reward to the person who finds it.'

The farmers searched every corner of the field, but in vain. The watch seemed to have disappeared. Just then, a small boy walked to the farmer and asked for a chance.

The farmer got irritated, 'Look, little one, neither these able-bodied young men nor I have been able to find it. How will a small child like you find it?'

The boy begged him for an opportunity to conduct his search. Since the boy kept persisting, the farmer finally relented. The boy went about his task and, within fifteen minutes, he returned with the watch in his hand. The farmer was overjoyed.

He asked the young child, 'None of us could find it! How did you manage to succeed?'

The boy replied, 'Most of you searched the field, but with a lot of commotion. I just went about my task silently. In the silence, I was able to hear the ticking of the watch. That helped me locate it!'

When your mind is at peace, you can achieve anything. An anxious mind is like being in a noisy place. In the above story, neither the farmer nor his friends were able to find the lost watch. This was because of the great commotion they caused during the search. The noise during the search ensured that no one could hear the ticking of the watch. As the object was small, none of them could see it in the huge field. However, the little boy had enough sense to realize that the only way a watch could be found in a massive field was by 'listening to it'. Doesn't the above anecdote reflect our everyday lives? In our current lifestyle, how many of us listen to the sounds of nature? Do we even have the time to think about it? Do we even realize what we are missing?

Bengaluru, until the 1980s, was known as 'Pensioner's Paradise'. Endowed with a salubrious climate, greenery, and low cost of living, it was a dream for every person to settle down in the city. Except for a few public enterprises, there were very few private industries in Bengaluru. It was a sleepy town where it was not uncommon to see deserted roads before 8 a.m. in the morning and after 8 p.m. at night. If you took a walk around 9 a.m. in the morning in any of the city's numerous parks, you could see hundreds of people walking on the jogging tracks, clad in tracksuits or traditional attire. One-hour walk in Lalbaugh—one of the oldest and most famous gardens in the city—ensured a loss of 100 calories, which was quickly followed by a visit to MTR—one of the oldest eateries of Bengaluru, where dollops of butter on masala dosa ensured that the weight remained unaffected! After a sumptuous breakfast, the man of the house would take a lazy stroll in Gandhi Bazaar to buy freshly plucked vegetables from the market. If you were one of those who preferred to spend the day lazing around at home, you could hear the chirping of sparrows, watch monkeys running playfully on the branches of nearby trees, and squirrels nibbling at nuts.

Unfortunately, the IT boom in the 1990s and 2000s changed all this. Majority of the lakes dried up, and greedy builders encroached upon these lands. Trees were cut to make way for roads and metro. Quaint cottages were replaced by monstrous skyscrapers. For a city that boasted of just one multi-storied building (aptly called 'MS Building'), it became a common sight to see apartments at every nook and corner of the bustling city.

These days, a majority of the roads experience huge traffic jams, resulting in incidents of road rage. During most part of the day, the roads in Bengaluru are clogged like the arteries of a man suffering from high cholesterol. The felling of trees and transforming lakes into concrete beds have resulted in fleeing of the lovely birds and animals. No longer do you hear the chirping of a sparrow or a cuckoo in the city. The poor animals and birds lost their habitat in this concrete jungle. Now, the only sound you get to hear is that of honking horns. It is a pity that a city, once known as the 'garden city' and 'air-conditioned city', is bursting at its seams and plagued by excess traffic, population and pollution today. A typical IT professional's day starts around six in the morning. After a hectic day, he comes home late at around 9 p.m. Even after his return, a quick dinner is usually followed by a series of telecons and Skype chats that continue well past midnight. Where is the time to sit in the living room and gaze lazily out of the window? Not that you can spot a sparrow or a monkey anyway!

In our jet-paced lives, it is very important to take breaks from our hectic schedules. Go for a long drive; spend your weekend at a 'natural' resort or a hill station. Drive away from the hustle and bustle of the city. Leave your laptop behind; restrict your mobile phone for only emergency calls. Cut off social media during these breaks. Take early morning treks. Watch the sunrise and follow the butterflies in the parks. Be one with nature and listen to the sounds of birds and bees.

Karma
(Action)

Karma, in Sanskrit, signifies 'action' or 'deed'. It is the act of performing one's duties without the desire of gaining anything in return. According to the theory of karma, just like every cause has an effect and every action a reaction, what we do in our lives comes back to us. Forgiveness, kindness, compassion, understanding, etc., are all a part of good karma, which produces positive outcomes for the individuals performing them. Give the world the best that you have, and the best will come back to you.

The Hospital Window

*Happiness is a hard thing because it is
achieved only by making others happy.*

—Stuart Cloete

Once an old man was admitted to a hospital. He did not have enough money to afford a room all to himself, so he had to share it with another patient. This room had two beds and the one next to the window had already been allotted to the other person. The old man, thus, had to settle for the bed that was next to the wall and away from the window.

Both the men were bedridden and unable to move much. Therefore, with little else to do, they began to talk. Soon the roommates discovered that they had both led very adventurous lives. Having started their lives in the army, they had moved to the corporate world. Both of them had married, had had children, and later grandchildren. They had toured around the world and visited beautiful places. Having led such king-sized lives, each of them had many interesting anecdotes to share. They sat and chatted for the whole day. Within a few months, they became inseparable. The only regret the old man whose bed was away from the window had was that he missed looking at all the wonderful things happening in the world outside. One day, he mentioned this casually to his companion.

'Don't you worry, my friend. Henceforth, I promise to describe all the beautiful scenes to you,' his companion assured him.

From then on, the man sleeping next to the window began

to describe everything that he witnessed from his window. The events varied. Wedding processions passing on the road, crowds dancing on the streets, monsoon rains falling on the window sills, whirlwinds creating a dust storm, autumn leaves falling on the ground, couples holding hands and kissing each other, and so on. He would talk about swans swimming in the lake, children playing in the garden. Each scene was different in its own unique way and similar as well—the underlying message being love and beauty.

The patient whose bed was next to the window was so good and descriptive at narrating the scenes that the old man felt as if he was actually witnessing these sights. He no longer missed the window of the hospital room. His neighbour was now his window to the external world. Many months passed. One day, the old man did not hear the usual chatter from the neighbouring bed. His companion appeared to be sound asleep. When his companion did not wake up even after a long time, the old man sensed something was wrong and alerted the nurse. The nurse came in and inspected the man. She sadly declared that the other patient had passed away. She pulled the blanket over his face and wheeled him out of the room.

The old man was heartbroken. He missed his talkative friend. He realized that his only companion now was the window. He requested the nurse to move him to the bed that was next to the window. The nurse agreed to oblige him. The old man was happy. He thought to himself, 'Now I can spend the rest of my life looking at the beautiful lake, park, flowers, wedding processions, young couples and children.'

As soon as he was moved to the next bed, he sat up and looked out of the window. Imagine his shock when he saw that there were no lakes with swans swimming in it, no lush green parks, no children playing in the park, and no couples holding hands. All he could see outside the window was a graveyard and drab grey gravestones.

He called the nurse and asked her, 'Where have the lakes and the parks vanished? Where are the pretty flowers? The children?'

The nurse calmly replied, 'Sir, ever since I have known, the neighbouring part of this building has always been a cemetery. The only people who go there are those who want to bury their dear ones. Occasionally, we have people visiting the cemetery with flowers for those graves.'

The old man was dumbfounded. How could it be true? What happened to all the beautiful things that his neighbour had described all these months?

He asked, 'If it has always been a cemetery as you say, then how was my neighbour able to see all those beautiful creations of God?'

The nurse smiled, 'Sir, I do not know what you are talking about. Your neighbour was blind for the last five years. He could not have seen any of those things. Maybe he was just trying to cheer you up.'

When we are young, our parents play a major role in our lives, which is filled with learning, happiness and peace. During our student days, all our needs are taken care of and we lead a carefree life. In most cases, it is only after we take our first step into adulthood that we begin to shoulder responsibility. When we were kids, our parents would often take us out on vacations to hill-stations, beach-resort, pilgrimages or historical places. Each of these places had its own uniqueness that filled our childhood memories with joy and happiness. These are golden moments we cherish throughout our lives.

As time passes and as we grow old, there is a role reversal. It is now time for us to plan holidays where we take our children and ageing parents along. It is our way of reciprocating the pleasures that we experienced during our childhood—of returning the joy of visiting new places, meeting different people, experiencing different cultures, relishing various cuisines, etc.

As our parents grow older, in most cases, they are troubled by ill health. Some of them get afflicted with diseases such as arthritis, heart ailments, knee problems, etc., that make travelling difficult. In certain cases, they are also bedridden. What do we do in such cases? Decide not to take them for a vacation, right? In majority of the cases, that is what we do. As a consequence, our parents miss out on all the fun they deserve. Wouldn't it be nice if we spent long hours with them after our trips, narrating our experiences to them?

Just imagine the pleasure that your parents would feel if you tell them about the rollercoaster ride at Disneyworld, Orlando, the skiing on Swiss Alps, or about playing with the dolphins at Sentosa Island, Singapore. In a digital era where we click thousands of pictures with our cameras or mobile phones, all it takes is a simple TV with a USB drive to make them experience our thrills and adventure. It is always nice to take your family to the most scenic and picturesque places in the world. However, when that is not possible, the next best thing is to help them live those experiences vicariously, through narration, videos or photographs.

The Starfish Story

Act as if what you do makes a difference.
It does.

—William James

On an early morning, a man was taking a walk on a deserted beach. The tide was receding, thus, exposing the wet sand. There was only one other person on the entire stretch of the long beach. He noticed the other person repeatedly bending down on the ground, picking up something and throwing it back into the sea. The man wondered what the other man was picking up and hurling back into the sea, and that too, in the early morning hour when the rest of the city was still asleep.

Finally, when he could no longer control his curiosity, he ran towards the other man, eager to find out what he was up to. As he approached the stranger, he could make out the object that he was throwing into the sea. They were beautiful starfish. When he asked the man what he was doing, he replied, 'Each night, the high tide brings these starfish here. As the day breaks, the tide subsides, and these poor creatures get left behind on the wet sand. All starfish you see have been washed onto the shore in a similar manner, and if they stay like this for a few more minutes, they will die due to lack of oxygen. I am throwing them back into the ocean and trying to save their lives.'

The man was not convinced by his reply. He asked, 'How does your throwing a few starfish back into the sea be of much help? There are thousands of them lying on this long coastline.

You cannot rescue all of them, can you? Also, there are hundreds of such beaches on the planet and each of them has thousands of such starfish. What difference can you make?'

The other man smiled. He bent down, picked up a starfish, and as he threw it into the sea, he said, 'For that one starfish, I made a difference!'

Each one of us is like the man on the beach. We come across hundreds of problems and think, 'What's the use of fixing just one problem? Will it make a difference?'

Yes, it will. For that one problem, you are the solution.

We may not be in a position to solve all the problems of all the people around us. However, like the person throwing the starfish into the ocean, we can convince ourselves that by solving a few of them, we can indeed make a difference—one at a time.

Take for example two of India's major problems—illiteracy and poverty. In a way, both these issues are linked to each other. People are illiterate because they have no money to go to good schools and, in turn, they are poor due to lack of education. We also have numerous other problems such as deteriorating environment, lack of proper infrastructure, poor sanitation and hygiene. Each one of us can play a role to minimize these problems. Unfortunately, everyone thinks, 'How can I single-handedly make any difference?'

India's literacy rate has grown to 74.04 per cent from 12 per cent, at the end of British rule in 1947. While this is a significant jump, we still have a long way to go; especially when we compare ourselves with some of the developed countries. Rather than thinking that it is our government's duty to eradicate illiteracy, why can't we play a role in its alleviation?

Just imagine what would happen if each one of us decided to teach just one unfortunate person? Won't we eradicate illiteracy in no time?

What prevents us from donating clothes and books to underprivileged children? I have seen many men spitting paan on the streets. When I ask them to stop, they say, 'Even if I stop doing this, what difference it will make in a huge country like India?' They might not see it, but it will surely make a difference.

Every night, after an early dinner, I go out for a long walk. I frequently come across people dumping garbage on the roadside. When I remind them of our prime minister's 'Swachh Bharat Abhiyan', they smile and reply, 'That's the prime minister's initiative. I am sure he and his supporters are working towards achieving it.' Yes, it is the PM's initiative, but it is definitely not a task that can be achieved by his men alone. Each and every citizen of the country has a role to play.

I helplessly watch people breaking traffic rules, especially during peak traffic hours. On numerous occasions, I have stopped my car and asked the traffic violator, 'What do you plan to do with the couple of minutes that you have saved? Why don't you follow traffic rules like the rest of us?' It is sad to note that in most cases, I get back an earful of swear words that cannot be mentioned here. The logic of these violators is similar to the paan-spitting men: 'How can one person make a difference?'

Let us discuss the starfish anecdote again. What if the stranger on the beach had thought like the people described above? What would have happened to the poor starfish that ultimately made it to the sea due to his kindness?

Well, as individuals, we can, and we should make a difference. There is a well-known saying: 'Little drops of water. Little grains of sand. Make the mighty ocean. And the beauteous land.'

The same is true for all philanthropic initiatives. Each of us can make a difference to another's life; just as the man did to the starfish. All we need to do is take the first step.

The Race of Life

*It is literally true that you can succeed best and
quickest by helping others to succeed.'*

—Napoleon Hill

This incident happened a few years ago at one of the Special Olympics. One of the events slated at the tournament was the '100-metre dash'. There were nine contestants for the race and all of them were mentally disabled. Soon it was time to start the race and, as in any normal race, all the nine contestants stood at the starting line, waiting for the start-shot to be fired in the air. All the contestants aspired to win. The competitive spirit was not lost on them.

When the gun was fired, the contestants dashed towards the finishing line. Suddenly, one boy stumbled in his tracks. He fell down and began to cry. He was upset that months of preparations would go waste. He knew that he stood no chance of even reaching the finish line, leave alone winning. The other eight contestants heard the boy sobbing. All of them stopped running and stood, looking at the boy who had fallen down. Soon, something unexpected happened. One by one, these runners began to turn back and walk slowly towards their fallen comrade. They stood around him and tried comforting him. A little girl even bent down and kissed him.

When the boy finally stopped crying, all the nine contestants held each other's hands and walked together towards the 'finish' line! Every spectator in the stadium stood up and gave a standing ovation to these gentle souls.

The phrase 'help others win' seems like an oxymoron, doesn't it?

The word 'help' is generally meant to refer to people who are 'in need'—those who need our support, who might be down in the dumps. Helping such people ensures that they are bailed out from the 'dungeon' and brought to the 'ground'. At no stage does it result in the person being helped to rise above the person who is helping, right?

Now let us analyse the word 'win'. When we say that A has won, it invariably means that A has outperformed the rest of us. So, when we say 'help others win', it means helping others to achieve as much as you have achieved or more. How many of us are willing to do that? A woman earning more than ten lakh rupees a year will happily donate a few thousand rupees to an NGO for the education of an underprivileged child. In fact, she would feel good about it, and rightfully so. A man who dines every day in the best restaurants in the city would be very happy to ask his cook to pass on the leftover food to a beggar at his doorstep. A girl who is a class topper would surely be willing to help a classmate who is struggling in his or her studies.

In all the three cases, the 'recipient' of the 'help' is far more underprivileged than the 'donor'. At no point in time does the 'donor' look at the 'recipient' as a competitor. There is no threat or challenge. The woman who earns a lot of money will not experience even a small dent in her savings if she donates a few thousand rupees towards the cause of educating an underprivileged child. The man dining at the finest restaurants will continue to do so, despite his cook giving leftover food to the beggar. The girl will continue to top in her class despite helping her struggling classmate.

Now let us tweak these case studies a bit. Would the woman

be willing to donate a few lakh rupees from her salary to help the underprivileged child? Would the man be ready to take the beggar with him to a five-star hotel and share the same table with him? Would the bright girl be willing to teach a classmate who is scoring just a couple of marks less than her? You know the answers to all the above questions. That is the reason why I stated that 'helping others win' is an oxymoron. However, isn't helping others, at the cost of your victory, a beautiful thought? Just think about it.

God made all of us equal at the time of our birth. We are all born from a womb and have come to this world empty-handed. At the time of our deaths, we again become equals since we return to the kingdom of God, empty-handed. If we come to this world and depart from this world in a similar manner, then why should all of us not lead our lives in a similar manner? Why is there a willingness to help others only to a certain degree? Why are we reluctant to make them as good, or better, than us?

In the Special Olympics anecdote, the children were differently abled. They were probably not aware of the impact of winning or losing. Prior to the race, they had been instructed to dash towards the finishing line. When one of them fell down, their priority was to help him rather than reaching the finishing line. For them, reaching the finishing line was not a 'goal', it was just a 'task'. Helping their friend was more important than reaching the finishing line.

Comfort Zone

The biggest risk is not taking any risk. In a world that is changing really quickly, the only strategy that is guaranteed to fail is not taking risks.

—Mark Zuckerberg

Thousands of years ago, there lived a tribe in the caves of South Africa. These people were known as 'cavemen' since they spent their whole lives in dark caves. These men and women were endowed with eyes like any normal human being but since they had never stepped out in light or used their eyes to look around, they had extremely poor eyesight. At the same time, as they had always stayed in the dark caves, they had not even seen each other.

The cavemen had never seen or used fire. They used to eat raw vegetable roots shrubs and leaves that grew in the darkness inside their caves. Winters were the toughest months because the temperature would drop drastically. The only way known to them to fight off the chill was to huddle together and use their body heat to keep themselves warm. Little kids and the older people would scream in agony. Despite the pain and sufferings, this was considered a normal practice since they did not know anything else.

On one such cold and chilly winter night, as the cavemen sat huddled together, they heard the sound of footsteps. At first, they thought it was a wild animal, but the sounds of the feet sounded more human. Before they could pick up their spears, they heard a human voice. The cavemen felt relieved that it was not a wild animal but a human being like them.

The stranger said, 'Don't worry. I am a person like all of you.'

After a brief silence, the chief cavemen stood up and directed his question to the voice coming from the dark, 'Who are you, stranger?'

The stranger replied, 'I come from a faraway land. I have come to help you.'

'Help us?' the chief was puzzled.

'Yes, help all of you. I know how troubled you all are due to the cold weather.'

'No one can help us. Every winter we experience such chilly nights. We just have to bear it!'

'No, you need not suffer like this. I have brought help.'

The chief and rest of his tribe remained silent. They did not know if they could trust a stranger who could read their minds. He reiterated that he was there only to help them. For the next few minutes, he neatly laid down piles of wooden logs. On top of the wooden logs, he placed stacks of dried leaves. The cavemen could just hear the rustle and this made them more restless.

The chief shouted, 'Hey stranger! What are you doing to us? What have you brought with you?'

The stranger did not reply. He silently went about his work. Soon, he lit the pile of wooden logs and dried leaves. Within a few seconds, the flames lit up the entire cave. Sparks flew all over. The cavemen had never seen fire. Nor had they seen light. They screamed in great panic, 'Stop it! What are you doing? It's hurting our eyes!'

The stranger smiled, 'This is fire. It not only keeps you warm and wards off the cold but also gets rid of the darkness that currently envelops your lives.'

The cavemen continued to howl and scream. They shouted

in unison, 'Stop it! We are unable to bear it. It is getting too hot for us to breathe! We will all die!'

The stranger once again smiled and said, 'I assure you that nothing like that will happen. You have never seen fire in your lifetime, and so you will need some time to get used to it. I know that the heat is too much for you right now. However, within a few minutes, your bodies will get accustomed to it.'

'No way! We won't come near you!' the cavemen shouted in unison.

One young lady, however, stepped out of the group. She walked towards the fire and stood next to the stranger. Initially, the fire seemed to burn her whole body. She screamed in agony.

'You are a fool to have believed the stranger. Now you suffer,' the chief admonished the young lady.

The stranger grabbed the lady by her shoulder and held her close to him. As his comforting hand caressed her long tresses, she began to feel much better. The fire wasn't bad after all!

She could not only see the handsome stranger but also started feeling warm and cosy on an otherwise wintery night.

'All of you should come closer to the fire,' she pleaded to her tribe.

However, her tribe was adamant. They refused to take a step forward.

'The stranger is right. Once you get used to the fire, you can see everyone. The fire will also dispel the cold,' she assured them.

'Shut up, young lady! Don't you dare make us fall into the stranger's trap,' the chief shouted angrily.

'No, chief! It is so warm and nice here. You just need to have faith,' she pleaded.

However, none of the cavemen stepped forward. They seemed content with staying huddled away in the darkness.

They preferred shivering in the cold rather than venturing into an unknown territory.

❖

The above anecdote is similar to the well-known 'frog in the well' story. The cavemen, who had lived in darkness all through their lives, had gotten quite used to it. They probably even loved it during summer.

We, too, like these primitive men, love to stay in our comfort zone. How many of us would like to move out of it? Haven't we refused job offers in a different city, even if the new job was better than the current one in most aspects? Haven't we refused new roles in our own organizations because it meant stepping out of our comfort zone? In most public-sector banks, the employees in clerical positions are not transferred from the city in their initial years. They get used to their branch office—their colleagues, their clients, the environment, etc. A few years into their service, they are promoted as officers. However, this comes with, what they see as, a huge 'drawback', because an officer's job is transferrable. This means that the stability of their clerical position is replaced by transfers to different cities across the country. It means relocating their families, moving their children to new schools, spouses having to seek a transfer and, above all, getting accustomed to new social and cultural environments.

In order to avoid all these challenges, some bank employees take the easy way out—they refuse the promotion and prefer working as clerks for their entire lives. It is quite sad to see professionals refusing promotions if it involves getting out of their comfort zone.

❖

Here is another interesting story.

Once a king returned from a faraway land with two beautiful eagles. None of his noblemen had seen such beautiful creatures in their lives. They stood admiring the magnificent birds. The king called his trainer and handed him the birds for training.

A couple of weeks later, the king asked the trainer about the progress he has made in training the birds. The trainer requested the king to accompany him. A few minutes later, the king and the trainer arrived in a huge field. The latter pointed towards the blue sky. On looking up, the king noticed an eagle soaring and gliding majestically in the clear skies.

The king asked the trainer, 'I think I had given you two eagles. Where is the other one?'

The trainer pointed his finger at a banyan tree and remarked, 'My Lord! Please look at the topmost branch.'

The king looked in the direction of the trainer's fingers and exclaimed, 'Yes! There is the second eagle. But why is he sitting so still?'

The trainer replied, 'My Lord, he has been sitting that way since the time you handed him to me. The first eagle has been flying high in the sky, but the second eagle seems content with just sitting atop that branch.'

The king was not satisfied with the answer. 'There must be a reason. Have his wings inspected. Maybe he has injured himself.'

The royal vet was summoned. He thoroughly inspected the perched eagle and ruled him fit. By now, the king was frustrated. He called the royal astrologers to find out the reason for the eagle's strange behaviour. The royal astrologers, too, could not solve it. Finally, the king consulted his chief minister.

His chief minister advised him, 'O Lord, Please consult a farmer.'

'A farmer?' the king exclaimed.

The chief minister explained, 'Yes, a farmer, my Lord. A farmer is someone who stays close to Mother Nature; he would know the behaviour of most animals and birds. Let us consult him.'

The king agreed. Next morning, the king, accompanied by the trainer, took a farmer to the banyan tree.

Pointing at it, he told the farmer, 'Look at the eagle sitting on that branch. He has been sitting like that ever since I brought him. Can you investigate and find out what the problem is?'

The farmer replied, 'O great King, please come back after thirty minutes.'

Exactly thirty minutes later, the king returned to the banyan tree. The bird was nowhere to be seen. He asked the farmer, 'What did you do to my beautiful bird?'

The farmer pointed towards the sky and said, 'O Lord! Please look there!'

The king noticed the eagle soaring majestically in the clear blue sky. He asked the farmer, 'What miracle did you perform? How did you make that bird leave its resting place and soar in the sky?'

The farmer smiled and replied, 'I just cut the branch on which the bird was resting!'

We all have the potential to fly but sadly, we do not realize it. We like to rest in our comfort zones, and just like the second eagle, we are not willing to discover our hidden potential.

Inertia and being in the 'comfort zone' are our biggest enemies. However, when we are pulled out of it, we are, after an initial struggle against fear of the unknown, able to unleash our true potential—just the way the second eagle did after the branch was cut.

Kindness

Sow an act and you reap a habit. Sow a habit and you reap a character. Sow a character and you reap a destiny.

—Anonymous

Once there lived an eighteen-year-old boy who did not have sufficient money to pay his tuition fees. One day, an idea occurred to him and his friend. They decided to host a music concert to raise funds for their education. They decided to invite the renowned pianist Ignacy Paderewski for the concert. When contacted, his manager demanded $2000 for the concert. Unfortunately, the two boys did not have that much money. Even after pooling in all their resources, they discovered that they could just manage $1600. They called the manager and told him that they would give $1600 in cash and the balance $400 in the form of a 'postdated' cheque.

A couple of days later, Paderewski invited the boys to meet him. He told the two young boys, 'I heard about your payment problem. This is just not acceptable.'

The boys' hearts sank. 'Sir, we will try to give the balance amount at the earliest,' they pleaded.

The great musician smiled. Tearing the cheque, he handed over the cash to the boys and said, 'Please deduct all your expenses from $1600. You can give me whatever amount is left. Also, you need not pay the remaining $400.'

The boys were thrilled and thanked him profusely. Years passed by. Paderewski went on to become the prime minister of Poland. He was a great leader, but his country was badly hit during World War II. Millions of people were starving in his country and he had no money to feed them. He realized that the only option was to seek help from the US Food and Relief Administration.

The US Food and Relief Administration was headed by Herbert Hoover. He agreed to help Paderewski immediately and shipped thousands of tons of food grains to the starving people in Poland. Paderewski was greatly relieved. He decided to personally meet Herbert Hoover and thank him on his country's behalf.

As Paderewski began to thank Hoover for his timely gesture, the latter interrupted and smiled, 'Sir, no need to thank me, please. You might not remember this. Many years ago, you had helped two young students to host a music concert. I was one of them.'

This is a tale of two great leaders—Paderewski, a pianist, became the prime minister of Poland and Herbert Hoover went on to become the president of the United States of America.

Generally, famous artists are known to not only be pricey but also quite stubborn about their charges. Knowing their true worth, they are seldom willing to compromise on their rates. Ignacy Paderewski was a different breed. He was touched by the boys' decision to give him 'postdated' cheques of $400. Having earned thousands of dollars, a paltry amount of $400 would not have made a big difference to him. Keeping in mind the boys' happiness and not wanting to disrupt the event, he agreed to do the event free of cost. The only amount that he charged was his own expense incurred for the event.

Once there lived a young boy who worked as a sales boy to fund his school fees. He would finish his school by 2 p.m., and spend the next few hours going from one door to another, selling his wares. One sunny afternoon, the poor boy was feeling tired and hungry. He had already visited more than fifty houses without any success. The scorching sun was making him weary and thirsty. He decided to quench his thirst by asking for water in the next house.

A beautiful young woman opened the door and invited him inside. After purchasing a few items, she smiled and asked, 'What would you like to drink?'

The boy felt relieved that she had offered him water before he had asked for it. 'A glass of water please,' he replied.

The young lady went inside her kitchen and returned a few minutes later. 'Here you go! Have a glass of milk,' she offered.

The boy hesitated. The young lady smiled and thrust the glass of milk into his hand. 'You look tired and thirsty. Please have this.'

The boy drank the entire contents in one long gulp. Giving back the empty glass to her, he asked, 'How much do I owe you?'

The lady smiled once again and replied, 'You owe me nothing. There is no price for kindness.'

The boy thanked her profusely and left the house. Many years passed by. The young lady became ill. None of the doctors in her small town could cure her. She was asked to consult a specialist in a big city hospital.

Dr Howard Kelly, one of the most famous gynaecologists in the US, was called to treat her at the hospital. He decided to give her the best possible treatment and cure her of the dreadful disease. Many months later, the lady was finally cured.

Though she was cured, she was worried about the huge

medical bills. She had been treated at one of the leading hospitals in an expensive city. The doctor who treated her was not only the best but also the most expensive in the country. Could she afford it? In the meanwhile, her bills were sent to Dr Howard Kelly. The doctor scribbled a note and sent it to the patient. The patient fearfully opened the envelope. Against the 'amount to be paid' column, the doctor had scribbled: 'Already paid in full with one glass of milk.'

Both these anecdotes clearly indicate that kindness has no price and any act of kindness must be done without keeping any expectations in mind. In the second anecdote, the young woman was touched by the tired and thirsty boy's plight. For a person who lived comfortably, she had absolutely no hesitation in feeding a needy child, and she even refused to accept anything in return. It is also important to note that in both instances, the donor had done a favour without keeping any vested interests in mind. Neither Ignacy Paderewski nor the young woman had any idea that they would later need help from the same person they had helped.

What Goes Around Comes Around

I am a true believer in karma.
You get what you give, whether it's bad or good.

—Sandra Bullock

A kind-hearted woman loved to feed the poor and needy. While cooking dinner, she always made it a point to keep a few extra rotis on the windowsill of the kitchen. She noticed that on most nights, a beggar would come and take away her rotis. The beggar never thanked her.

Instead, he would pass a cryptic comment, 'Whether you do evil or good, it finally comes back to you!' This happened every day. The woman would expectantly await the arrival of the beggar, and the latter never disappointed.

The woman was quite puzzled at the beggar's remark. One day, she asked the beggar, 'Everyday, you pick up my rotis, instead of thanking me, you utter a cryptic statement and walk away.'

If the woman expected an answer from the beggar, she was disappointed. The beggar just repeated, 'Whether you do evil or good, it finally comes back to you!'

A few more weeks passed. The beggar never thanked her for the food. By now, the woman was beginning to lose her patience. 'Why should I feed this ungrateful person? Let me kill him!' she thought to herself. With these thoughts, she poisoned the rotis that she had prepared for the beggar. As she was about to keep the rotis on the windowsill, her hands began to shake.

She regretted her deed and felt angry with herself.

'What am I doing? I keep the rotis to feed the poor and the needy, not to get accolades from them. Why should I fish for compliments?' she thought to herself. Thinking thus, she threw away the poisoned rotis in the dustbin and prepared fresh rotis. Within a few minutes, the beggar came to her doorstop. He picked up the food and said, 'Whether you do evil or good, it finally comes back to you!'

A few hours later, there was a loud knock on her door. She was surprised to find her son standing at the doorstep. His clothes were torn and his body was covered with bruises. Moreover, he had gone to war and was not expected to return so soon.

The woman asked her son, 'How come you are back so soon? Isn't the war still going on?'

Her son nodded his head and replied, 'Yes, the war is still going on. However, I was injured and asked to return. While travelling in the army truck, we were ambushed by our enemies. They blew up the truck but I somehow managed to escape. Due to my leg injury, I had to limp my way back to the army base camp. I was injured, tired and famished. Luckily, I met a beggar on the way. This kind-hearted soul not only took me to his hut, he even treated me with delicious rotis. That was the only food that he had with him. He sacrificed his own meal to feed me. I would have died, had it not been for the kind beggar.'

Hearing this, his mother collapsed on the sofa. She remembered what she had done earlier in the evening. She had poisoned the rotis and kept them on the windowsill. Had she not replaced them, her own son would have eaten the poisoned rotis and died! It was at that moment that she fully understood what the beggar told her every day: 'Whether you do evil or good, it finally comes back to you!'

❈

Many years ago, I worked for an American multinational. There, I used to interact with two Business Unit (BU) Heads; let us call them Manager A and Manager B.

Once we had a major organizational reshuffle that resulted in many groups moving across different BUs. Manager A had to shift a major group to Manager B. Manager A, being a cunning person, cleverly handed over the group to Manager B, but with a different set of project managers. He retained all the good project managers in his remaining groups and filled the group that he had to hand over with poor-performing project managers. Manager B complained that he had unfairly been given the projects with a different set of project managers. Unfortunately, their boss sided with Manager A, and hence Manager B ended up with a high number of non-performers.

A couple of months later, Manager B quit the organization. We had another round of organizational reshuffle that resulted in Manager A taking over the BU that Manager B had handled so far. All the non-performing project managers under Manager B now became part of Manager A's headcount. During the farewell lunch the management team hosted for Manager B, the latter was quick to sarcastically tell Manager A, 'You gave me all the rotten apples. Now sit and eat them!' Just imagine what would have happened if Manager A had handed over all the good project managers to Manager B, since they rightfully belonged to the latter. Manager A would have ended up inheriting some of the best project teams in the organization.

Why are we so hesitant to hand over our 'goodies' to others? Especially in situations where they become the rightful owners, as we saw in the above example? In the cases of Ignacy Paderewski and Dr Howard Kelly, we saw kind-hearted gestures being reciprocated in an equally nice manner. In the roti anecdote, the woman tried to cause harm to a beggar and almost ended up killing her own son. Hence, we should understand that whatever we do, it finally comes back to us one day.

No Expectations

If you give a good thing to the world, then over time, your karma will be good and you will receive good.

—Russell Simmons

One night, an old woman was travelling in a car from Mysore to Bengaluru. Normally, it was her husband who drove the car, but this was not just another day. Her sick husband was sleeping beside her. He had to be taken to a good hospital in Bengaluru and the only option for her was to drive.

The car was just a few miles away from Channapatna, a small town famous for wooden toys. The old woman was feeling weary and hungry. She had not eaten anything since morning. It was worrying her since she was diabetic and skipping meals could affect her health and well-being. She was not used to driving on the busy Mysore–Bengaluru highway, and the heavy traffic was adding to her stress.

'Let me quickly grab something to eat in Channapatna before I proceed to Bengaluru,' she thought to herself.

Suddenly, she heard a squeaky noise and found her car slowing down. She brought her car to a halt and got down. She noticed that one of the tyres was flat. Oil was leaking from the car. Though she had a spare tyre in the trunk, she had absolutely no idea how to change tyres and fix oil leakages. Her only hope was to get help from fellow travellers on the highway. The old woman stood beside the car and waved at all the vehicles that passed by. None of them stopped. They either did not notice her small, frail figure or they did not care. As minutes went by, she grew restless and frustrated. Just when she was about to give up, she noticed a taxi slowing down and stopping a couple of feet away from her. The taxi driver got down from the car and walked towards her. Though he was shabbily dressed, with an unshaven face and unkempt hair, he had the most charming smile she had ever seen.

'What's the matter, madam? Your car has broken down?' he asked.

'Yes, flat tyre and oil leakage,' she replied.

The young man smiled cheerfully and said, 'Why don't you rest for a while, madam? I will fix it.'

The woman stared at the shabbily dressed man and hesitated. She was not sure if she could trust the stranger. As if reading her mind, the young man smiled and said, 'Don't worry! My name is Kumar and I have come to help you.'

Hesitatingly, the woman got into the car and Kumar began working. He removed the spare tyre quickly from the trunk and, using the jack, he pulled out the flat tyre. Within ten minutes, the tyre was replaced. Next, he opened the bonnet. Flashing his pocket torch at the engine, he quickly identified the oil leak. He removed his handkerchief from his pocket and tied it at the leakage. It was not perfect but would serve the purpose.

Meanwhile, the old woman had dozed off. Suddenly, she heard someone knocking at her window. It was the young man who had helped her with the car repair. As she got down from the car, he smiled cheerfully and said, 'Madam, everything is fine. The tyre has been replaced. The flat tyre is now inside the trunk. Though the oil leakage has been fixed temporarily, I suggest that you take it to a garage for repairing.'

The woman looked relieved when she said, 'I don't know how to thank you! I just cannot imagine what I would have done without you. My sick husband is sleeping in the car and he needs medical attention. Had it not been for you, I would have spent the entire night on the highway.'

The young man replied, 'Had it not been me, it would have been someone else!'

'How much should I pay you?' the woman asked. She noticed that the young man was already walking back towards his taxi.

'Pay me? Nothing! I didn't help you with an intention to charge money,' the young man sounded hurt.

The woman put her hand on his shoulder and replied gently, 'I know you didn't do it with an intention to make money. However, I am sure you need some money.'

He noticed the old woman staring at his tattered clothes. The man smiled once again, 'I am sure you will find someone needier than me. Give this money to that person.'

Saying this, he walked away. The woman got into her car and slowly drove towards Channapatna. A few minutes later, she noticed a small roadside restaurant next to a petrol pump. She was famished. She quickly stopped her car and went inside the restaurant while her husband slept in the car.

The restaurant was small and crowded. It was teeming with travellers who were on their way to Bengaluru. With great difficulty, she managed to find a chair for herself. All the waiters seemed to be busy taking orders. She could not help noticing the waitress who finally came to take her order. The waitress looked extremely tired and was walking with great difficulty. It had been a very hectic day for her, like most of her days. Her clothes appeared dirty and soiled. However, she still had a cheerful smile on her face. It immediately reminded her of Kumar, the kind man who had helped her on the highway.

The old woman placed her order, and the food was served promptly. She gobbled the food since she had to proceed to

Bengaluru quickly. She also got something packed for her husband. The waitress handed over a bill of ₹200. The old woman was struggling with her purse. The waitress had to process the orders of many other impatient customers, so she quickly went back to the kitchen. When she returned to the table, she noticed that the old woman had already left. On the table lay two notes of ₹500 each. She was sure that the old woman had gotten confused.

'She has kept ₹1000 instead of ₹200. Let me rush to the car park and return the balance amount to her,' she thought.

As she was about to leave the table, she saw a handwritten note: 'You need not return the balance amount. I wanted to give this money to a person who helped me. He refused to take it and told me that I must give it to someone needier than him. And I think that person is you.'

The young waitress had tears in her eyes. She picked up the money and went back to work. She could not wait to narrate this incident at home. For the next couple of hours, she was busy taking orders, serving food and clearing tables. She completely forgot the incident that had happened a few hours back. Finally, as the restaurant closed its shutters for the night, she walked towards the car park. She knew her beloved husband would be there to pick her up as usual. Her husband had already arrived at the car park. Placing the notes in his pocket, she flung into his arms.

'I have the most fascinating story to tell you, Kumar,' she wept with joy.

It is important to remember that whatever we do finally comes back to us. In the above anecdote, the old woman wanted to pay Kumar for helping her. However, he refused to take the money. He deserved the money for helping her out, so it ultimately came back to him.

When we help someone, we should always do it without any expectations. That is the reason why I get irritated when certain NGOs, while seeking donations, inform me, 'Sir, your donation is exempted from income tax.'

To me, the decision is based on the credibility of the NGO and not whether I get a tax exemption or not. Are you donating because you want to help someone or are you doing it for tax exemption?

A few months ago, I attended a workshop on CSR (Corporate Social Responsibility). The presenters boasted of providing industrial education, installing lathes in workshops, providing farming equipment, distributing subsidized fertilizers, etc. At the end of two intense hours of presentations that seemingly had a huge impact on the social sector of the country, the head of one of India's leading NGOs was asked to speak. The head made a very powerful statement.

He remarked, 'It is very heartening to see so many companies coming forward to contribute towards the cause of the poor. However, I would like to know how many of these initiatives were done without keeping a "vested interest" in mind. For example, the industrial education was provided to the people in town X because the company wanted to subsequently hire them in their shop floor...'

The speaker went on to prove that in more than 90 per cent of the cases that had been presented, the corporates had started initiatives in the social sector keeping their commercial interests—such as cheap labour, inexpensive crops, etc.—in mind. While it is good to see corporates contributing in the area of social sector, would it not be great to see them contribute in areas that are not in their line of business?

Bridging the Gap

*How people treat you is their karma;
how you react is yours.*

—Wayne Dyer

Once there lived two brothers in a village. They both owned adjacent farms. From sharing toys and bicycles as children to sharing machinery, equipment and water supply as adults, the two shared a great rapport. By optimizing their resources and infrastructure, they made handsome profits each year.

Unfortunately, personal rivalry and greed soon took over. They had a bitter fight and after that, things were never the same. The two not only stopped speaking to each other, but they also stopped sharing their resources. This resulted in a sudden drop in profits. Though both the brothers knew the reason for the declining profits, their egos did not allow them to admit defeat. They preferred to maintain distance rather than accept the reality.

One bright day, there was a knock on the elder brother's door. He found a carpenter standing at his doorstep. The carpenter said, 'Sir, I am jobless and looking for work. I am a highly skilled carpenter. Please give me any task and I will exceed your expectations.'

The elder brother thought for a moment and replied, 'Yes, I think I have a job just for you. Please follow me.'

The carpenter followed the farmer who took him to the gate of his farmhouse.

The farmer said, 'Can you see that creek over there? And

the farm beyond that? Well, that farm is owned by my younger brother. Until recently, there was a beautiful lush green meadow between our farms. One day, we had a fight. In anger, my brother mowed down the lovely meadow. Now we have an ugly creek separating our farms.'

The carpenter asked, 'What do you want me to do?'

The farmer laughed and said, 'I want to return the favour. Please purchase logs of wood and build a fence around my farm. A very high fence. Ten feet tall; so that I do not have to see his farmhouse! Let us see how he responds.'

The carpenter said, 'Yes, sir. I understand your requirements. I will go the market right away and purchase all the raw materials. I should be done with the fence in a couple of days.'

The farmer replied, 'I am going out of town for a few days. I hope to see the fence when I return.'

The carpenter nodded his head.

The farmer was thrilled. Whistling with joy, he returned home and began to pack for his journey. Thinking of his brother's reaction made him laugh heartily. The carpenter went to the market and purchased some wood. He spent the next two days cutting and sawing wood and going about his task. Finally, it was complete and he was greatly relieved.

Meanwhile, the farmer returned home. He was shocked at the sight. There was no fence in front of his house. Instead, a wooden bridge lay on the creek. Before he could turn to the carpenter and scold him for disobeying him, he heard a loud shout.

He turned around and noticed his younger brother running towards him. Crossing the newly laid bridge, his younger brother flung into his arms and wept, 'Oh, brother! Please pardon me! How foolish and immature have I been! You have shown me the way. I took a bulldozer and destroyed the beautiful meadow between us, but you reciprocated by building a bridge. Please forgive me.'

The older brother was astounded. He looked at the carpenter who was busy packing his toolkit. He did not know how to thank the carpenter.

'Wait, you must stay with us for a few days,' the older brother exclaimed.

The carpenter winked and shook his head, 'No! I have many other bridges to build.'

It takes many months to build a bridge, but just a moment to destroy it. The two brothers had a fallout that later resulted in the younger brother destroying the meadow between their homes. The elder brother was eager to retaliate by building a fence around his home. Had he done that, his younger brother would have done something similar or worse, and their differences would have never been sorted. What would they have gained other than satisfying their bruised egos? Nothing. What would they have lost? Everything.

Luckily, the elder brother met the wise carpenter. He not only knew how to build bridges, but also believed in Mahatma Gandhi's words: 'An eye for an eye makes the whole world blind.' It is quite common to have a misunderstanding with our close friends or family members. Rather than distancing ourselves, we should try our best for reconciliation.

I have known many cases of friends turning into foes. During the initial phase, both abuse each other and cut off all links. Later, they indulge in one-upmanship, where each one tries to outperform the other, usually in a harmful manner. Finally, there are long periods of cold war. Both parties have hurt written all over their faces. Even if they have done sufficient introspection to realize their own mistakes and faults, they do not want to accept them. Though both know that reconciliation is the best option, their egos do not allow that.

When you are separated from another individual by ten feet, the only way you can meet is to walk five feet in the other person's direction and hope that the other person will do something similar. However, we seldom do that. We endlessly wait for the other person to make the first move. In many cases, an entire lifetime is lost in waiting.

Have you ever taken the first move while trying to patch up a broken friendship or a relationship? Have you noticed that when you take the first step and apologize for your mistake, the other person not only forgets your mistake but also confesses all his faults and asks for forgiveness?

Try it the next time and you will see the difference.

Team

*Coming together is a beginning;
keeping together is progress;
working together is success.*

—Henry Ford

One of the oldest management lessons related to teamwork can be learnt from geese. We might have often wondered why these intelligent birds always fly in a 'V' formation. When each goose flaps its wings, it creates an uplifting force for the goose flying immediately behind it. When they fly in a 'V' formation, they are able to cover around 70 per cent more distance than flying individually.

When a goose falls out of the formation, it begins to feel the air drag. The air resistance increases and it begins to tire. It knows that the only way to continue is to get back into the 'V' formation. Keen observers will notice that when the first goose gets tired, it indicates with its wing. Another goose takes over as the tired goose shifts to the back of the formation.

It is also common for the geese at the back to be noisier than those in the front. But actually, what seems like noise is actually the sound made by the geese to encourage the geese in the front! The most amazing sight occurs when a goose is injured or is no longer able to fly. When it begins to fall out of the formation, two other healthy geese leave the formation as well. Their prime responsibility then becomes to protect and take care of their sick friend. Once their sick friend recovers, all of them wait to join the next 'V' formation that flies their way.

While it is always an amazing sight to watch a geese formation flying in the sky, there are many lessons to be learnt from this. The most important lesson is the meaning of TEAM—'Together Everyone Achieves More'. As stated earlier, when the geese fly in a 'V' formation, they can cover 70 per cent more distance than when flying alone. This is true in our lives too. In games involving teamwork—such as cricket, football, hockey, or basketball—we have seen numerous examples of mediocre players coming together, playing as a high-performance team, and winning prestigious tournaments. In the corporate world, too, we have seen both types of instances—a team of average individuals achieving results beyond everyone's expectations through great teamwork, and cases of star performers faring rather poorly as a team.

When a goose at the front begins to tire out, it realizes that it is going to slow down the entire flock. It does not want its weariness to affect the team's performance. Rather than sticking on as a leader in the front of the formation, it happily hands over the baton to a younger and more energetic goose and retires at the back.

I wish humans were also as generous and content as the geese. Unfortunately, most of us are not. Even in the game of cricket, we have so many examples of star players sticking on well beyond their prime and, in the process, damaging the reputation they worked so hard to build.

Kapil Dev is hailed as the greatest all rounder India has ever produced. He was a match winner for India with both the ball as well as the bat. However, in his eagerness to break the record of Richard Hadlee, he ended up playing fifteen extra tests that he shouldn't have. For a person who used to consistently take five wickets in an innings, he struggled to get even two wickets in an innings towards the fag end of his career. The media and the spectators wanted him to retire. Though he finally managed to break the record of Sir Richard, his reputation was in tatters. The other fallout of Kapil Dev's extended career was the delayed entry of Javagal Srinath in test cricket. Considered as the fastest bowler that India has ever produced, Srinath had to warm the benches and watch the greatest Indian all-rounder struggle on the field.

The other classic case is that of another cricketing legend, Sachin Tendulkar. When India won the World Cup in 2011, it was probably the right time for him to retire. It had been his dream to win the World Cup for India and he had achieved it. Unfortunately, some cricket enthusiasts discovered that Sachin was just short of scoring a century of centuries in international cricket. While this was a meaningless piece of statistics (combining test record with ODI record), the entire nation went gaga over it, including Sachin Tendulkar. Despite poor performances in matches against England and Australia, where we were mercilessly thrashed, he stuck on. After struggling to achieve this inane record, we then witnessed his desire to achieve a landmark of 200 tests.

We also have a great cricketer who behaved just like a goose. Just one failed series and that too against the best cricketing nation in the world made Rahul Dravid realize that it was time for him to hang up his boots and make way for younger players.

When the head goose indicates that it is tiring, one of the geese is immediately ready to take over. Similarly, in corporate life too, we should be ever willing to stand up for others. When the call of duty beckons us, we must be ready to lead. When one of our colleagues fall sick, how many of us stop our work and take care of his/her work? I once overheard a group of executives discussing their sick colleague, 'Wow! Isn't it good that he has fallen sick! He is now going to miss out on his deadlines and it will affect his year-end rewards and recognition.'

There might be a few who would be ready to help, but with vested interest. I know of an instance where a manager asked his team members, 'X is sick and won't be coming to office for the next few weeks, so can one of you handle his tasks?' A majority of them refused, citing reasons of work pressure and lack of bandwidth. To the manager's relief, one person agreed. However, imagine the shock that the manager had when, a few days later, that team member walked into his cubicle and whispered, 'Sir, I hope I get rewarded and compensated adequately for the extra tasks that I have been handling.' When we are lagging behind in the team, it is very easy to get demotivated. Our immediate thoughts might be, 'When I am lagging behind, how does it matter if my team wins or not?'

Thankfully, geese do not have such a pessimistic attitude. Those at the rear end of the 'V' formation continuously encourage those in the front.

Take the Plunge

*The only limit to your impact is
your imagination and commitment.*

—Tony Robbins

There lived an old farmer in a small American town. Due to his ill health and old age, he needed his son's help in farming. One day, the son was arrested by the police for committing petty crimes in the neighbourhood. The father was shattered. Who would help him with his daily chores now? Farming involved a lot of physical work, and his frail health did not allow him to work as much as he would have liked to. Since his son was imprisoned in the neighbouring town, he had no means to personally meet him. His communication with his son was restricted to exchanging letters.

The season to grow potatoes was fast approaching. He did not have the strength to dig his farm, so he wrote to his son, 'The potato season is about to commence. Every year, you would help me in digging the field. I do not know what to do this year. Shall I hire a few contract labourers? Please suggest.'

Within a couple of days, he received the following letter from his son, 'I am so glad you asked me for my suggestion. Please do not hire anyone for digging up the farm. I have hidden a few guns there before I landed in jail.'

Within a few hours, a truckload of army men landed in his farm. The next few hours, they were busy digging up the farm. The sophisticated metal detectors could not detect any guns. Frustrated, they left his farm after dusk. The old farmer who had been watching the proceedings since morning was completely confused. He wrote another letter to his son, describing the day's events.

A couple of days later the farmer received the following letter from his son: 'Now that the army has done my work, please go ahead and plant your potatoes! This is the best help that I could provide from here.'

There are millions of people who are well placed in life and want to do well to others. They feel the desire to give back to the society. While these noble thoughts are good to hear, the actual execution is a different story altogether. While many people want to serve the society, very few people actually end up doing it. Have you ever analysed the reason for such low participation? Well, there is no paucity of thoughts or funds. The only thing lacking in people is their willingness to take the first plunge.

I have known many people expressing their desire to help the underprivileged, but they never actually do so. They want to move from the corporate sector to the social sector, but it rarely happens. When I question them about their 'desire' versus 'execution', their responses are:

'I am not sure if I should take a plunge at such an early age', 'Will it pay me enough to take care of my family?', 'How do I know that the NGO is not a fraud?' and 'Can I join the corporate sector at a later date?'

A few friends of mine wanted to start a 'foundation' to fund the NGOs. While this was an excellent thought, it remained just that. When I asked them about their plans of starting the much talked about 'foundation', most of them replied, 'I will start once I have sufficient money to take care of my family.' Unfortunately, they could never gauge what 'sufficient money' was, and so, they could never get started.

In my opinion, all these are moving targets. We never seem to have enough money to take care of our families. We never seem to have a bank balance that gives us comfort. The only way to get into the social sector is to take a plunge.

In the above anecdote, when the father wrote about growing potatoes, his son did not express any kind of helplessness. His responses could well have been: 'I wish I could have helped', 'I am stuck in jail, so what can I do?', or 'I will help you as soon as I am out of the prison', etc.

However, he said none of this. Without putting too much thought into it, he directly plunged into action. His quick and 'out-of-the-box' thinking helped him solve his father's problem despite being locked up in a jail in the neighbouring town. If you decide to help someone, you can do it, no matter which part of the world you are in, no matter what your present condition is.

Niyati
(Destiny)

Niyati means destiny. But destiny, in this case, is not chance. Instead, it is the outcome of our choices. The only person we are eventually destined to become is the person we decide to be. We can create our own happiness. Rather than being trapped in trivial issues, we should try and look at the bigger picture. Everyone wants to achieve quick results without worrying about the consequences. Fortune will play its role, but only we can decide what we want, when we want it, and how we can achieve it without causing harm to others.

Rat Race

The foundation stones for a balanced success are honesty, character, integrity, faith, love and loyalty.

—Zig Ziglar

Once there lived a successful businessman who had no children. As he aged, the question of choosing a successor came up. In the absence of a natural heir, he decided to hand over his business to the best executive in his company. The businessman had a difficult time choosing the right person, because all his front line executives were equally competent in their line of business.

'There's not much to differentiate among them. What do I do?' he thought to himself.

After a lot of thinking, he had a brainwave. He called his top ten executives into the boardroom and said, 'I would like to find a worthy successor for myself.'

All the executives were anxious to know who would be chosen. Seeing the expression on their faces, the businessman said, 'Don't worry! I am not going to announce that today. I will hold a competition, and the winner will be made the CEO.'

When asked to elaborate further, the businessman gave a seed to each of his executives and said, 'Take this seed home and plant it in your garden. I would like each of you to nurture it well with good soil, manure, water and sunshine. At the end of the year, I would like you to bring your plant to office. The person with the best plant will become the CEO.'

There was silence in the room. Each executive was thinking the same thing: 'How can I become the CEO?'

All of them narrated the incident to their family members in the evening. Each said, 'I will put in all efforts to nurture this seed into the most beautiful plant and become the CEO.'

A few days later, the executives met in the office canteen and, as expected, the conversation veered towards the topic of seeds. Most of them said that they had buried the seed in a pot and some of them even mentioned that they were able to see the first shoots sprouting out of the soil.

Ram—one of the young executives—was worried. He had himself planted the seed and mixed the best manure to the soil. Unfortunately, the seed had not yet sprouted any leaves. That evening, he narrated his worries to his wife. She hugged him and said, 'Don't worry, my dear! Since no two seeds are the same, some seeds might take a few extra days to sprout.' Feeling reassured, he fell asleep.

A few weeks later, the executives once again met in the canteen. Each of them boasted about their plant and how great it looked. Ram was worried. He had nothing to talk about. His seed seemed to have gone into a deep slumber. That night, he once again expressed his frustration to his wife. She smiled and consoled him, 'Don't be impatient. I am sure things will work out.'

Once again, feeling comforted, he went to bed.

A few months passed. The executives continued to brag about their plants. Only Ram remained silent. He had nothing to contribute to those discussions. Slowly, he was beginning to lose confidence in his wife's assurances. 'I am doomed,' he thought to himself.

Finally, a year went by. The businessman called his executives to the boardroom and instructed, 'Tomorrow morning, I will meet all of you here at 10 a.m. sharp. I would like each of you to show me your plant.' Ram went home feeling sad and dejected. He did not want to go to office the following day. His wife comforted him again and said, 'Don't worry. Please take the empty pot and explain it to your boss. I am sure he will understand.'

Reluctantly, Ram took the empty pot to his office the next day. He got the shock of his life when he entered the boardroom. All the other executives were chatting animatedly. Each of them was standing next to a beautiful plant. Ram entered and stood at the farthest corner of the room. 'Hopefully, the CEO will not notice me if I stand here,' he thought to himself. Soon, the businessman walked in. He beamed and greeted everyone. He shook each executive's hand and praised the plants that the executives had brought. Finally, he approached Ram.

Looking at the empty pot, the puzzled businessman asked him, 'Why have you come with an empty pot?'

Ram looked embarrassed. He noticed everyone looking at him intently. He decided that confessing the truth was the best option. The moment he narrated his tale of woes, the businessman smiled and patted his back sympathetically. The businessman swiftly moved to the front of the room and announced, 'I have evaluated all of you and I am pleased to announce that the winner is Ram!' Everyone in the room, including Ram, was shocked. They wondered what Ram had done to deserve this.

One of the executives gathered courage and asked, 'Why have you chosen Ram? He was not even able to grow a simple plant. How do you expect him to grow this company?'

The businessman smiled and replied, 'Exactly a year ago, I had given each of you a seed. In reality, it was a dead seed. No plant could have sprouted from those seeds. All of you cheated me by bringing plants that had not grown from the seeds I had given. Only Ram was truthful. His courage to accept defeat and his honesty made me choose him as the new CEO of this company.'

In today's rat race to achieve success, we find most people taking shortcuts to reach their goals. How many of us—be it in school, college, or the corporate world—really want to wait and slowly climb the ladder of fame and glory? In the above anecdote, the businessman wanted to find a worthy successor. Having founded and led the business himself for many years, he felt that the person leading it in the future should be able to run the enterprise based on the values and principles he had built it on.

The businessman had a strong management team, which had very good credentials in terms of revenue generation, technology and innovation, customer satisfaction, employee engagement, etc. They were all very good at their jobs. In the end, the only key differentiator that he noticed among his executives was in the field of ethics and values.

When the task was given by the businessman, every executive wanted to win the challenge. They felt that compared to some of the tough and gruelling assignments they had faced, this was the simplest. Just plant a seed, water it, nurture it, and you have a beautiful flowering plant! However, the executives received a rude shock. Without realizing that they were dead seeds, they began to panic. They thought, 'How do I grow this plant? I can't let this dead seed ruin my chances of becoming a CEO!'

We are all born honest and innocent like Ram. However, as we face the rat race to achieve success—during our childhood and youth—there is a high possibility of our value system being corrupted. Rather than investigating and thinking about our failures, we take the easy way out. We display someone else's achievements as ours and hope to fulfil our ambitions through such actions.

So, the next time someone wants you to grow a plant, first inspect the seed that you have been given.

A Tale of Two Cats

*The most dangerous phrase in a language is,
'We have always done it this way.'*

—Grace Hopper

One day, a tourist visited a Buddhist monastery in Nepal. While he enjoyed the serenity and ambience of the place, he was quite surprised to observe a strange tradition. Before the prayers began, two young monks brought two cats and tied them to a banyan tree right opposite the prayer hall. Curious about this tradition, the tourist decided to visit the monastery the following day as well. He once again noticed this unusual tradition being repeated. Unable to contain his curiosity, he decided to ask the monks about this strange tradition. Unfortunately, all the monks were observing 'maun vrata' (a vow to keep silent), so he did not get any response from them. Disappointed, he returned to his hotel and decided to visit the monastery the next day.

On the third day, the prayer was delayed by a couple of hours. When he asked one of the monks about the delay, he explained, 'This is because we are unable to find any cats.' The tourist asked curiously, 'What do you mean?'

The monk replied, 'You might have observed that we tie two cats every day to that banyan tree. Unfortunately, we are unable to find any cats in the monastery today. So, a couple of monks have gone in search of cats in the town. Once they return with the cats, we will start with our prayers.'

'But why are the cats tied to the banyan tree?'

The monk shrugged his shoulders and replied, 'I have no

clue. It is a tradition that we follow here.'

A few minutes later, the monks returned with a couple of cats. They tied them to the banyan tree and asked everyone to enter the prayer hall. The prayer had been delayed by two hours just for the cats. After the prayers, the tourist met the two monks who had brought the cat and asked them, 'Oh, holy men! Please tell me the reason for tying the cats to the banyan tree.'

The monks replied in unison, 'We don't know since we are new here. We are just following the instructions. Please ask our head monk.'

The tourist was now getting restless. He had to solve this mystery. He rushed to the head monk and repeated the question. The head monk smiled at him and said, 'My child, this is an age-old tradition of this monastery. Our job is not to question why. We follow the instructions of the Lord.'

'But there must be some reason for tying cats to the banyan tree, right?'

The head monk was agitated and replied, 'I told you that we don't question our traditions. Go away now, you fool!'

By now, the tourist had lost all hopes of getting an answer. He returned to his hotel and narrated the story to the receptionist.

The receptionist suggested, 'Ten miles from here is a hill. A hermit lives there in a small wooden hut. Some say that he is 100 years old. Others say he is 200. Well, honestly, no one knows his real age. Please go and meet him. He might know the story behind this strange tradition.'

The tourist thanked the hotel receptionist and immediately left for the hill. He knocked at the door of the ancient hut. A few minutes later, an old, frail man slowly opened the door.

'What do you want? What brings you here?' he asked the tourist.

The tourist narrated the strange episode he had witnessed for three consecutive days at the Buddhist monastery. Hearing this, the old man began to laugh uncontrollably. The tourist was surprised at his reaction. He asked the old man, 'Sir, do you know the story behind this ancient Buddhist tradition?'

'What story? What tradition?' he laughed, and added, 'Many decades ago, a couple of kittens entered that Buddhist monastery. The monks living there took good care of them. The kittens were served milk and bread every day. However, as they grew older, they became very mischievous. They would run around the entire monastery, occasionally breaking the items kept on the floor. The monks had trouble while performing their prayers. Hence, it was decided to tie those two cats during prayer time. This became a daily ritual.'

The tourist listened to him attentively.

The old man continued, 'A few years later, those two cats died. However, by then, this had become a tradition. The old head monk, who had started the tradition of tying the cats to the banyan tree, had also died. The young head monk, who took his place, was not aware of the logic behind tying the cats. He insisted that his fellow monks should fetch two cats and tie them to the banyan tree. Only then he would start the prayers.'

It was the tourist's turn to laugh. 'The prime reason for tying the cats was to control them. However, when there were no cats left in the monastery, what was the logic behind fetching two cats from the town and tying them to a tree?'

The old man said, 'No logic, my son. This is what happens when we follow traditions without ever questioning them.'

I have lost track of the number of times I have questioned my father about some of the rituals, and his answer is always the same: 'This is the way we have always been doing it.'

In certain communities in India, when a person dies, his close relatives bathe. This tradition probably made sense many years ago, when people stayed in joint families. When a man died, his family members would perform certain religious rites at home and then visit the cremation ground for the last rites. It was felt that a visit to the cremation ground was an unhygienic task and this probably resulted in the family members taking a bath immediately after returning home. However, in today's world, such joint families are rare. If a person dies in Bengaluru, there is a high possibility that his relatives live in Brisbane or Birmingham or Boston. However, the tradition continues—the moment the news of the death in Bengaluru travels everywhere, his relatives in Brisbane, Birmingham and Boston rush to the bathroom!

In offices, too, people are slaves to tradition. Many years ago, the communication bandwidth used to be quite expensive and limited. This also meant that high traffic on the Internet slowed down the communication traffic considerably. Precisely, for this reason, most companies gave limited or no access to Gmail, Twitter, YouTube, Facebook and other social networking sites. Thanks to modern technology, we have high-speed Internet connections and, these days, communication speed and traffic is no longer an issue. With considerable progress in the field of 'search engine optimization' and social media, Internet has now become the best means of communication, especially in areas of marketing and publicity. In this context, it is unfortunate to see a few companies still taking the conservative approach of restricting social media to their employees. In addition, their excuse is always the same: 'Because we have always been doing it this way.'

Realizing Your Strengths

*Once we realize the extraordinary power we have to
compose our lives, we'll move from passive,
conditioned thinking to being co-creators of our fate.*

—Jason Silva

Kerala is a land famous for its temples, beaches, backwaters and elephants. Once a tourist visited the famous temple at Guruvayoor. As he roamed around its premises, he found an area that housed the temple elephants. The tourist noticed a strange sight. Ten elephants stood in front of him and each had a small rope tied to its leg. The other end of the rope was tied to a wooden peg fixed to the ground. The huge animals could easily break free but they did not.

He asked a mahout resting nearby, 'Are my eyes deceiving me? Are these elephants just tied to these small ropes?'

The mahout replied, 'Sir, what you are seeing is perfectly all right. The elephants are being held by the ropes and wooden pegs.'

'Is that strong enough?' the tourist asked.

'No, it's not,' the mahout replied casually.

Seeing the puzzled look on the tourist's face, the mahout explained, 'When these elephants were young, we used to tie them with the same ropes and pegs. At that time, these were all that was needed to hold them. However, these ropes and pegs are no longer strong enough to hold these huge creatures.'

'So why don't they break free?' the tourist was still puzzled.

The mahout replied, 'That's because they don't know their own strength. They have been conditioned from a young age to believe that it is not possible to break free.'

There is a similar anecdote about ten flies and a glass jar. A man took a glass jar and put ten flies into it. He quickly covered the jar with a colourless cellophane paper. Since the cellophane paper was colourless, it was invisible to the flies. Thinking that the bottle was open at the top, they tried to fly out, only to find themselves hitting against the cellophane paper. This went on for a couple of hours. Soon, the flies realized that they were trapped in the glass bottle and there was no way out. They could just fly inside the bottle. The flies, being intelligent enough not to injure themselves, would fly till an inch below the cellophane paper and then fly down. This way, they managed to avoid hitting themselves against the cellophane paper lid.

What do you think happened when the man removed the cellophane paper after a couple of hours? Do you think the flies flew out? No, they did not. Instead, they continued to fly until an inch below the cellophane paper and then move downwards. None of them flew out of the jar!

What do we learn from these two anecdotes?

In the first anecdote, when the elephants were young and weak, they did not have sufficient strength to overpower the rope and the peg. Therefore, after a few attempts, they gave up. As they grew older, they grew in strength too, and developed the power to pull the ropes off the pegs. However, they never made such an attempt because they did not realize their own strength. Their potential was never utilized and they preferred to remain tied to the pegs.

In the second anecdote, the flies could not escape the glass bottle due to the cellophane paper lid. In fact, they quickly concluded that they can never fly out, and so they did not even attempt to fly out after the lid was removed. This was another story about unrealized potential.

This is not just the case with elephants and flies. It happens with humans too. Most of us are like the elephants. When we are young, we quickly judge our capabilities and limitations and create a mental picture of how we perceive ourselves. We are quick to decide what we can do and what we cannot. This picture is firmly stuck in our minds until we die. Seldom do we see people trying to change their perception about themselves. Aren't there many occasions when we refuse to perform certain tasks because we do not know our own strength? In most cases, isn't this hesitation due to our childhood upbringing?

You would rarely find someone say, 'Hey, I know I couldn't do it five years ago. Let me try to do it now.'

Most people would say, 'I had tried it in the past and it hadn't worked. I know it never will.'

This happens because we are not ready to assess our strengths every now and then, just like the tied elephants. In a way, we are also like the flies. Once we receive a nasty blow on our heads, we quickly conclude and draw inferences that stay with us forever. Had the flies studied the situation after a couple of hours, they would have realized that the lid was no longer there and then they could have easily flown out. Similarly, if we keep assessing a situation periodically, we will know when the winds of change begin to blow favourably in our direction and when we can reattempt it. Unfortunately, we seldom do that. The moment we face such a situation, we say, 'I know this won't work. I have tried it before.'

A successful person is someone who keeps assessing his/her strengths and the situation periodically.

Wheel of Fortune

*There is a sufficiency in the world for man's need
but not for man's greed.*

—Mahatma Gandhi

Once upon a time, there lived four poor Brahmins in Ujjain. Drowned in penury, they were unable to take care of their wives and children. One day, one of their wives told her husband, 'Why don't you go to the famous temple of Lord Shiva and pray to Him? He is all-merciful. I am sure he will help all of us.'

The four Brahmin friends were greatly impressed with the idea. Next morning, they went to the temple of Lord Shiva and prayed to Him for wealth. As they came out of the temple, they met an old priest. He was chanting slokas near the temple gate.

'Oh Brahmins! What brings you all here?' he asked them.

When the Brahmins narrated their story, the priest took pity on them and asked them to accompany him to his home. The Brahmins agreed and followed him. The priest went inside his home and a few minutes later, he came out, holding four lamps. The Brahmins looked puzzled.

The priest smiled and said, 'These are no ordinary lamps. They have divine properties and the ability to find wealth. Please place these lamps on your heads and walk in the direction of the Himalayas. If the lamp falls on the ground, it means there is treasure nearby. Please dig the surrounding areas and I am sure that you will find wealth.' The four Brahmins thanked the old priest and started walking in the direction of the Himalayas.

After they had walked for a couple of hours, a lamp fell

from the head of one of the Brahmins. He dug up the nearby area. It turned out to be a copper mine. He was thrilled to find so much copper in one place. He filled his sacks with sufficient copper and told his three friends, 'There is sufficient copper for all of us. Please take whatever you want.'

The three friends refused and replied in unison, 'We want to proceed further since we hope to find something better. You may go home if you like.'

The first friend agreed and turned towards his home, while the other three friends continued their journey. After they had walked for three hours, another lamp fell down. He dug up the nearby area. It turned out to be a silver mine. He was thrilled to find so much silver. He filled his sacks with sufficient silver and told his two friends, 'There is sufficient silver for all of us. Please take whatever you want.'

The two friends refused and replied in unison, 'We want to proceed further since we hope to find something better. You may go home with this wealth.'

The friend agreed and turned towards his home. The other two friends continued their journey. After they had walked for four hours, a lamp fell from the head of one of them. He dug up the nearby area. It turned out to be a gold mine. He was thrilled to find so much gold in one place. He filled his sacks with sufficient gold and told the other friend, 'There is sufficient gold for both of us. Please take whatever you want.'

The other friend replied, 'Each time we proceed, we find something better. The first person found copper, the next person found silver, and you found gold. I hope to find something more precious and valuable.'

The friend who had found gold asked, 'What can be more valuable than gold?'

'I don't know. I want to proceed and find out.'

'All right then. I will wait for you here. Please go and try your luck.'

The fourth friend agreed and continued his journey. Slowly and steadily, the path became tougher. It was filled with sharp rocks. They began to cut his foot. Blood began to ooze out, but he was not disheartened. He continued his journey. As he moved ahead, the path became extremely steep. After five hours of walking, he suddenly heard a deafening noise. When he walked ahead, he found an injured man lying down in scorching sunlight. His body was full of wounds. Pus and blood was dripping from his limbs. His hair was dishevelled and his clothes were tattered. A giant wooden wheel was constantly spinning on his head, generating the piercing noise.

The Brahmin was shocked. 'Who are you and why are you lying in this state?' he asked the injured man.

No sooner had the Brahmin asked this question, the wooden wheel moved from the injured man's head to his head. He fell on the ground and his body began to bleed.

The injured man explained, 'I was also a greedy man like you. I found a gold mine but my greed made me go beyond that. My journey finally took me atop a steep hill. When I reached the top, I heard a strange buzzing sound. On following that sound, I discovered an injured man lying on the ground. A wooden wheel was rotating on his head. When I asked him about the wheel, it flew and hit my head. I have been lying in this manner ever since.'

'How long will this wheel rotate on my head? When will I be able to get up from this scorching heat? When will I be able to free myself?' the Brahmin asked, crying.

The injured man smiled and said, 'When another greedy person like you comes and asks you a similar question.'

This is a story of four greedy men or, perhaps, a story about most of us. The first Brahmin found enough copper to make all of them rich. However, the other three were not content with copper. They wanted to see what they could discover ahead. When the second Brahmin found silver, he too offered to share his wealth with his friends, but they once again refused his offer. Gold is considered as one of the most precious metals on earth. However, the fourth Brahmin was greedy enough to denounce even that. He wanted to find something more valuable. Though there is nothing wrong in having a desire to become rich, we should realize that there is a very thin line between ambition and greed. We should clearly understand the difference between what we need and what we want, only then can we lead content and peaceful lives.

Choices

*To give real service you must add something
which cannot be bought or measured with money,
and that is sincerity and integrity.*

—Douglas Adams

Once there lived two carpenters, Vishal and Vikram. They worked for one of the biggest contractors in the city who, over the years, had bagged all the prestigious constructions. The contractor knew that those two carpenters were the prime reason for his success. In an era when most contractors excelled in cost and delivery, it was the work of the duo that stood out. People loved to buy homes from him because they were rich in exquisite woodwork. It was as if Vishwakarma, the celestial carpenter, had himself done the work.

However, like all good things, this too had to end. Both of them were approaching sixty and wanted to retire. They told the contractor about their decision. Though the contractor felt sad to lose two of his best men at the same time, he agreed to their wishes. One day, as Vishal and Vikram were completing their final assignments, they received a phone call from the contractor. He asked both of them to come to his office immediately. They wondered the reason for the same as they walked in his office. The contractor smiled and shook their hands.

'Both of you have served me loyally for many years. Your work is recognized all over the city. I have one final wish before both of you depart. May I request you to please extend your stay and build just one more house each?' he asked.

Both the contractors looked at each other and remained silent. The contractor continued, 'I know that you have given commitments to your respective families. However, if you could just extend your stay for a few months, it would be very kind of you.'

The carpenters agreed to his request.

'Good. Let us start work from tomorrow itself,' the contractor suggested.

Both Vishal and Vikram started working on their new assignment from the following day. Vikram put in immense effort into his new project because he wanted to retire on a high note.

'My boss should know that I am the best in business,' he thought to himself. Tirelessly, he burnt the midnight oil. He even worked on the weekends, as he had to adhere to stringent deadlines. Finally, when the house was ready, it was one of the best in town. Each room had a different design. The wood used in each room was also different, as per the requirements. Ebony, rosewood and teak were used in the right places.

Unfortunately, the assignment meant something completely different for Vishal. He had mentally resigned from the contracting company. When his boss had assigned him his last project, he had unwillingly accepted the offer. 'My boss knew I was planning to retire. What was the need to assign me with this project?' he thought bitterly.

He allowed his team to go ahead with the work. Instead of inspecting their activities, he spent his time lazing around in his home. In the absence of any supervision, his team used inferior wood and created a shoddy design. The house turned out to be one of the worst projects of his career.

Both the carpenters completed their last projects on the

same day. When they went to meet the contractor, he was thrilled to see them. He hugged them warmly and said, 'I am so grateful that both of you were kind enough to take up these last assignments. Thanks for heeding to my request. Now here is a surprise. The house that you built is my gift to you!'

Saying this, he handed them the keys of the house that they had just completed. Vikram was thrilled to hear this. He had become the proud owner of one of the best houses in town. Vishal was crestfallen. He had landed a house filled with shoddy carpentry. Had he known that he was building his own house, he would have surely built it differently.

In the corporate world, most employees have their goals set by their managers at the beginning of the year. The next twelve months are for executing those goals. The employees put in their best efforts towards meeting the goals because they know that they will be evaluated based on them at the end of the year. However, if your manager was to tell you in October, 'I would like you to perform an additional assignment. However, it will not be part of your goal evaluation and performance evaluation.' What will be your immediate reaction? How will you perform in this additional assignment? Since the new assignment is not a part of your set goals and objectives, you will perhaps respond to the manager with a complete lack of interest. Your immediate reaction will be, 'Since this is not in my goal sheet, let it take the lowest priority. Let me finish all the other assigned tasks and then see what is to be done about this.' Since you already have set goals with timelines that were established at the start of the year, chances are that you will not have any time to execute this additional task. Even if you had the time, you might not have the inclination to put in your best efforts. There is a high possibility that you will end up doing a shoddy job, just like Vishal.

When you are executing the goals set by your manager, never have thoughts of 'what is in it for me'. The moment you have such thoughts, your quality of work will suffer. As Lord Krishna rightly preaches in the Bhagavad Gita, 'Put in your best efforts and leave the results to God.'

Both Vikram and Vishal had been excellent carpenters throughout their lives. They were the most sought-after carpenters in the city. It was very difficult to decide who was better of the two; such was their talent and workmanship. However, their true test came towards the end of their career. While Vikram treated this last assignment with utmost sincerity, Vishal treated it with disdain. The result was there for all to see. Vikram ended up spending the rest of his life in the most beautiful home in the city, whereas Vishal ended up being burdened with the biggest regret of his life.

Second Fiddle

Everyone has a role, and if you act within the parameters of your role,
the whole pack succeeds, and when that falls apart,
so does the pack.

—Jodi Picoult

The moon has been a symbol of love and romance for hundreds of years. In the beginning, it was believed to be a source of light. However, later, astronomers and physicists discovered that the moon was a celestial body that, unlike the sun, was not a source of light. It was also discovered that the moon merely reflected the sun's light on earth.

For thousands of centuries, the sun and moon worked in tandem, displaying excellent teamwork. While the sun shone on earth during the day, the moon shone at night when the sun had set, and when the earth would have otherwise been engulfed in darkness. Many poems and songs were written and sung about the beauty of the moon and its moonlight. For millions of earthlings, the moon appeared to be a source of soothing light. Unfortunately, all good things come to an end. One day, a star met the moon and poisoned his ear.

'Do you enjoy being the moon?' the star asked.

The moon was surprised at such a strange question. 'Yes, of course! Why?' he asked the star.

The star remarked, 'Tell me about your relationship with the sun.'

The moon explained, 'The sun and I share the most beautiful relationship in the universe. He is the source of all energy. His light and heat is responsible for the well-being of the entire plant and animal life on earth. If there was no sun, there would be no life on earth. The sun is the most important celestial being in the cosmos. He...'

The star interrupted, 'Enough! Enough of what the sun does! Let us talk about you. Tell me about your role in this relationship.'

The moon proudly replied, 'I am as important as the sun. While the sun provides sunlight during the day, I shine at night and prevent the earth from being engulfed in darkness.'

The star laughed, 'As important as the sun! What a joke. You do not even have your own light. You reflect the sun's light on earth.'

The moon protested, 'The earthlings find me beautiful and romantic. There are more poems written about me than about the sun.'

The star laughed once more, 'Earthlings are fools. They don't seem to be aware that you just reflect the sun's light.'

The moon was angry. He asked the star, 'What are you trying to say?'

'You are just a dummy. You just shine the sun's light on earth. Do you have anything to call your own? How long will you play second fiddle to the sun?'

The moon thought for a moment. There was some logic in what the star was saying. Wasn't he a dummy? Hadn't he been playing the second fiddle for too long? He asked the star, 'What should I do? Please advise me.'

The star replied, 'Stop playing second fiddle to the sun. Stop reflecting his light. Start generating your own light and let the earthlings see your true self.'

The moon agreed to follow the star's suggestion. He decided to compete with the sun rather than live in his shadow. The moon informed the sun that it was no longer interested in reflecting its light. The sun remained calm and just smiled back at the moon. Unfortunately, the moon was no match to the sun's beauty. It had a dull complexion and its body was full of craters. It did not know how to get rid of its ugly patches. It tried to change its appearance, but in vain.

After the moon turned away from the sun and stopped reflecting its light, the earth and earthlings suffered. The moment the sun set after dusk, there would be total darkness across the planet. People were afraid to walk around at night. The waves in the seas and oceans that depended on the moon were also affected. The disruption of high tide and low tide began to affect sea life. Millions of fish and seaweeds died. It was not just the earth that was affected adversely. The moon, too, was not enjoying its new role. Unable to generate its own light, it became an invisible body, like millions of others in the universe. Humans stopped admiring and praising the moon. It no longer remained the symbol of love, beauty and romance. It did not take long for the moon to realize his folly.

'I enjoyed such a harmonious relationship with the sun for thousands of years. Unfortunately, I came under the evil influence of a star. I should have remained happy assisting the sun, since it was how I, too, fulfilled my role and received glory. Instead, I became greedy and egoistic. I was stupid enough to believe that I could beat the most powerful and brilliant object in the cosmos,' it began repenting.

The moon went to the sun and wept, 'Oh, forgive me! I have been such a fool. For millions of years we shared a beautiful relationship. You were the source of all energy in this solar system. The entire earth depended on you and so did I. I was basking in your glory. Unfortunately, my ego fogged my thinking. I decided to compete with you, without knowing the futility of it all. I broke away my relationship with you.

However, you handled my tantrums with such maturity. You continued to shine on earth and protected all earthlings.'

The sun just smiled and said, 'Let's work together once again.'

Relieved, the moon instantly agreed. It got back its warmth and glow. People once again began to admire it and its light. Sea life thrived and the planet once again became a safe place to live in. The moon realized that at times playing second fiddle could be more satisfying than challenging the leader.

This is what lies at the bedrock of successful teamwork. It is important to understand that each of us has a role to play, however important or unimportant it may seem. It is critical to understand that we should derive the fullest satisfaction in executing that role. The moon had remained satisfied with its role for millions of years until a scheming star poisoned his ears. He rebelled. But after the initial euphoria of 'being different', it was a downward spiral for the moon.

Let us take another example from the game of cricket. If we look at the Indian team over the years, we will observe that there was a time in the 1990s and the 2000s when Sachin Tendulkar dominated the cricketing scene and was rated as the best batsman in the world. Rahul Dravid, despite being technically more accomplished, had to be content with being overshadowed by the exploits of his swashbuckling teammate. In a way, he played second fiddle to Sachin Tendulkar. Tendulkar, during his initial cricketing years, was simply brutal in his attack. He treated the fastest bowlers and the greatest spinners with equal disdain. He succeeded in hitting a six in the first over of a cricket match. Dravid never tried to match that. He was very happy to take a single and give strikes to Tendulkar. Statistics have shown that Rahul had a record of accomplishment as enviable as that of Sachin, and not just in test matches but ODI too. If Tendulkar was the 'sun' of the Indian cricket (high energy, great power), then Dravid was the 'moon' (gentle, intelligent). He was almost as unnoticeable as the moon, but as important as the sun. It was this perfect synergy between the two that gave the Indian team many memorable victories.

Sharpen Your Axe

*Give me six hours to chop down a tree and
I will spend the first four sharpening the axe.*

—Abraham Lincoln

Once upon a time, there lived a very poor man in a village. He was illiterate so no one was willing to give him a job. He also had no land for farming. In the same village lived a priest whom everyone respected. He was old and wise and had a solution to every problem. Most villagers consulted him when they faced any kind of hurdle. The poor man, too, decided to meet the village priest and seek a solution to his miseries.

One day, he came to the village temple and waited patiently for the priest to finish his daily rituals and prayers. The priest noticed the poor man waiting for him in the temple courtyard. After completing his prayers, he left the altar and walked up to him.

'What brings you here?' he asked.

'O wise one, you know everything, but you still ask me? I am poor. I am illiterate. I am unable to get a job and feed my family. Please tell me what to do.'

The priest noticed that the person standing in front of him was young and had a well built physique.

'Can you do manual labour?' the priest asked.

The poor man replied, 'O Holy One! I am ready to do any kind of work.'

The priest smiled, 'That's good. God always takes care of everyone. Follow me.'

Saying this, the priest walked out of the temple courtyard to a barn nearby. The poor man followed him. The priest opened the barn and went inside. A few minutes later, he came out with a huge axe. He handed the axe to the poor man and said, 'Please keep this with you. This will be your tool for survival.'

Seeing the puzzled look on the poor man's face, the priest explained, 'You are still young. You are endowed with a good physique. Our village is in the middle of a forest. The wood industry is the biggest employer in our village. I recommend that you become a woodcutter.'

The poor man was thrilled to hear this. He bowed in front of the temple priest and left in search of a job. The next morning, he presented himself at a wood processing company. He was hired immediately. His supervisor told him, 'We do not have a fixed salary here. We pay each woodcutter on the basis of the number of trees he cuts.'

The poor man nodded his head and left for the forest. After a hard day's labour, he managed to cut twenty-five trees. In the evening, he informed the supervisor about this. The supervisor accompanied him to the forest. After his inspection, he paid the poor man for his labour. The poor man was thrilled. For the first time in many years, he had a job. The next morning, he once again went to the forest and chopped twenty-five trees. He was once again paid for his work by the supervisor. On the third day, the woodcutter could cut only twenty trees. He was not worried.

'Just one of those days,' he consoled himself. The next day, too, he managed to cut only twenty trees. On the fifth day, it became worse. He could cut only fifteen trees. By the end of the first week, he was not able to cut more than ten trees. He spoke to his wife about it.

His wife replied, 'I think the priest cheated you.'

'What do you mean?'

'He told you that his axe was capable of chopping up to twenty-five trees per day. However, after a week, it could chop just ten trees per day. Who knows what will happen a week later?' she said.

The woodcutter comforted her, 'Let me go to the temple right away and meet the priest. He should be able to explain this.'

Saying this, the woodcutter rushed to the temple. He found the priest busy with the morning prayers. He barged in and shouted, 'You have cheated me!'

The priest turned towards him and asked him with surprise, 'What brings you here? You look very agitated and angry, my child.'

'Yes, I am. Your axe is not working. Please take it back.'

The priest was confused and asked the woodcutter to elaborate on his problem. The woodcutter narrated the drop in the number of trees that he could cut with each passing day.

The priest asked, 'During the past week, how often did you sharpen the axe?'

'Sharpen the axe?'

'Yes, tell me the number of times you sharpened the axe.'

The woodcutter replied sheepishly, 'Um... I was so busy with all the chopping and cutting that I had no time to even think about it.'

The priest patted his back and said, 'My child, how can you expect to have the same output from a tool that has deteriorated over time?'

Isn't this true in our lives too?

We are so busy cutting the trees that we rarely think of

sharpening our axe. While it is good to keep ourselves busy with the mundane tasks of daily existence, it is equally important to reserve time for honing our skills for the future. In an era where extracting maximum work from employees is the top priority of most organizations, competency ramp up takes a back seat. Every employee is loaded for 100 per cent of his time, so where is the time for his development? A lot of this depends on the culture of organizations, including their billing models.

Many years ago, I used to work for a Dutch multinational company. Like most software MNCs in India, it was a captive development centre for its parent organization headquartered in Europe. The company had a business model that encouraged billing its engineers on 'FTE' (full-time engineer) basis. This meant that we were paid per engineer, irrespective of what he did for the project and his workload. The teams in India were fully empowered to plan the activities of their engineers.

The project managers would plan for around 70 per cent of the engineers' time. The remaining 30 per cent was reserved for non-project activities such as training, competency development, participation in organization improvement activities, participation in various taskforces, etc. This kind of planning proved extremely beneficial to the engineers and, in turn, to the organization. The company was aware of its short-term, medium-term and long-term roadmaps. This ensured that its employees were trained on both operational as well as strategic competencies. They were geared up to handle complex projects with cutting-edge technology. Within a few years, a young team of coders and testers were able to transform into a competent set of architects and designers.

When the organization commenced its India operations in 1995, it was handed menial tasks. A few years later, our parent organization gave us better work. The big bosses in

Eindhoven noticed our competency ramp-up. Within five years of commencement of our operations, we were given 'full responsibility' projects. For certain products in the field of consumer electronics, we were doing 100 per cent of the product development. From a resource augmentation centre to a full-fledged innovation campus in five years was no mean achievement.

A few years later, I had an opportunity to work in another MNC that was both similar and dissimilar to the earlier one in many ways. While it was also a captive development centre for its European headquarters, it had a very different business model. The Indian engineers were billed on 'hours worked for the project' and not 'FTE'. This meant that the more hours the engineer worked on the project, the more money the company made. In today's world where revenue generation is everybody's priority, the project manager would load the engineers completely (100 per cent). No time was reserved for the engineers to develop or increase their own competency.

The net result was there for everyone to see. While the company was doing quite well in terms of timelines and quality of its deliverables, it remained a supplier rather than evolving into a key partner. Even fifteen years after the company had started its operations in India, there was no change in the kind of work that was assigned to the Indian engineers. Thanks to an inappropriate myopic billing model, the engineers never evolved to move up the value chain.

In the first company, the engineers were allocated sufficient time to sharpen their axe. This benefitted the Indian engineers and development centre. In the second company, the engineers were constantly chopping trees with no time for sharpening their axe. This led to stagnation of the engineers and the organization.

The House on Fire

There is an unseen life that dreams us; it knows our true direction and destiny. We can trust ourselves more than we realize and we need have no fear of change.

—John O'Donohue

Once, in the city of Mangalore, there lived a fisherman. His house was close to the Ullal beach. Every morning, he would go fishing in the Arabian Sea and return in the evening. Having faced many storms in the sea, he had become an expert sailor.

One day, however, the storm that broke out was too strong for him and his boat. The ferocious waves crashed against his vessel and smashed it into a hundred pieces. The fisherman caught hold of one of the drifting pieces of the broken boat and somehow saved himself. It was evening and he was hungry and tired, and in no time, he slipped in a deep slumber. All night long, the makeshift raft wafted aimlessly in the high sea. When he woke up in the morning, he discovered that he had drifted hundreds of miles away from Mangalore. He found himself travelling towards an island. As soon as the broken boat reached the island, he jumped out and ran towards the land. The fisherman was thrilled to discover land.

'Let me quickly go to the *Telegraph* office and send out a message to my folks back home. Then I will go to the harbour and organize a boat to return home. But first, I need to grab something to eat. I am famished, let me hunt for a restaurant,' the fisherman thought. He wildly ran around the island. It was surrounded by thick vegetation. It barely took him thirty minutes to discover that there was not a soul on the island.

'Gosh! This island is not inhabited. How am I going to establish communication with my folks? How do I return home?' he thought anxiously.

The next few days were very difficult for the fisherman. Having lived a sheltered life in Mangalore and being accustomed to the basic necessities of life, he found it difficult to survive on the island. Instead of cooked rice with sambhar, he had to now rely on raw vegetables and fruits. There were no more hot water tubs for his bath or cushioned mattresses for sleeping; instead, he had to depend on the cold and brackish waters of the Arabian Sea for washing himself and had to sleep on a makeshift pad of coconut leaves under the open sky.

As days passed by, the fisherman began to get used to the vagaries of nature. He survived the afternoon heat, the heavy rains and the chill of the night. Each morning, he prayed to God to be rescued. However, his prayers seemed to go unanswered. Meanwhile, the marooned fisherman had learnt to build a hut using the materials that were available in abundance on the island—stones, sand, coir, dry leaves, etc. The hut allowed him to take shelter from the blazing afternoon sun and rainy nights.

One day, there was a forest fire on the island. His hut and a few surrounding trees were caught in the blaze. He had no proper tools to douse the fire. He tried using empty coconut shells, but all was in vain. Within minutes, the entire hut that he had assiduously built was razed to the ground. The poor fisherman had not only lost his residence but all his possessions that he had stored in it. He was shattered. Initially, the fisherman was upset with the forest fire for having destroyed his belongings. Later, he shifted his wrath towards God.

He looked heavenwards and screamed, 'Oh, God! Why are you giving me such misery? First, you broke my boat and marooned me on this island. You separated me from my near and dear ones. I had no proper food or shelter. Just when I was getting used to this a solitary life, you came back and destroyed whatever little I had! Why me, God? Please answer me!'

Overcome with emotions, the fisherman fell on the ground and began to weep inconsolably. He did not realize as minutes flew by. He lay on the ground cursing his fate. Suddenly, he saw a shadow near his face. He looked up and discovered a man standing next to him. He was wearing the Indian Naval Guards' uniform. The fisherman was shocked. It had been more than seven months since he had seen a human being.

'Who are you? What brings you here?' he asked.

The man smiled, 'We belong to the Indian Naval Guards. Our duty is to protect the coastline of India. We undertake sea voyages frequently and ensure that there are no trespassers.'

The fisherman was still puzzled, 'How did you find me today? I have been here for many months now.'

The man in the uniform explained, 'We passed this island many times but didn't stop by since it is uninhabited. Today, however, we saw a hut on fire and that made us suspicious. We knew that someone must have been residing here. Hence, we came to this island to investigate, and found you.'

There are many instances in our lives when we feel our prayers are not answered. However, we should realize that our prayers get answered eventually, just at an appropriate time. There are occasions when we are struck by natural or man-made calamities. First, we are in denial, followed by anger and helplessness. Finally, once we overcome our troubles, we experience joy. These are repeated cycles, just like the one experienced by the fisherman.

Initially, when the fisherman was stuck all alone at sea, he was in the denial mode, unable to come to terms with the fact that fate had been cruel to him. This led to anger and a feeling of helplessness. However, it soon changed to joy when he discovered an island. On reaching the island, his mood quickly changed. He discovered that the island was not inhabited. Once again, he went into the denial mode and felt angry and frustrated. However, after a few days, he learnt to adjust with the available resources on the island. Slowly, he began to experience joy and peace once again. However, the day his hut caught fire, the cycle repeated itself. Initially, he was in the denial mode. He was unable to believe that all his efforts of constructing a hut with limited resources had been futile. This led to anger and frustration, resulting in helplessness. Luckily, his fortune changed for the better. Seeing his burning hut, the alert team of Indian Naval Guards rescued him.

This happens to all of us. We are continuously in a cycle of ups and downs, caught in the 'Wheel of Fortune', also known as 'Kalachakra'. Only when we realize that anything that goes up has to come down and vice versa, can we experience true bliss and happiness.

Assumptions

Destiny has two ways of crushing us—
by refusing our wishes and by fulfilling them.

—Henri Frederic Amiel

There once lived a poor old man in a village near Amritsar. Since he was not employed, he hardly had any money to feed himself and his family. However, all the villagers envied him because he owned a beautiful white horse. It was the most majestic-looking horse in the entire kingdom. Many rich noblemen asked him to sell his horse. They would say, 'We will shower you with money. You can repay all your debts and lead a comfortable life.'

However, the old man would always refuse this proposal, 'The horse is like a son to me. Does anyone sell his son? Even in poverty?' Saying thus, he would send away the prospective buyers.

One morning, he noticed that the horse was not in its stable. He complained to the village headman. The headman chided him, 'You fool! You did not listen to any of us. So many of us were willing to buy your horse for a huge sum of money, but you refused. Now you have been robbed off your horse and have lost everything. You are so poor that you are unable to take care of yourself, let alone take care of your horse. You should have realized that without proper shelter and protection, your horse would get stolen.'

The old man replied, 'Please don't pass judgements and draw your conclusions so soon. At this point, all we know is that the horse is not in its stable. How can you assume that it is stolen?'

The headman replied, 'Can't you see that it is stolen? You are a gullible fool.'

Other villagers heard the conversation. They laughed at the old man's foolishness. They always considered him to be a fool because he had refused to sell his horse and lead a comfortable life. He had no money to feed his family but continued to be stubborn. This stubbornness had resulted in this situation.

A few days later, the horse returned. It not only came back to the old man, but also brought ten other horses with it. The old man was naturally thrilled and told this to the other villagers.

The villagers remarked, 'How lucky you are! You proved us wrong. You not only got back your horse but now have ten new horses.'

The old man was quick to reply, 'Please don't conclude that I am lucky. I just told you that I have ten new horses. Let us wait and see if I am indeed lucky.'

The villagers said, 'You have eleven beautiful horses. What more could you want?'

The old man chose to remain silent. A few days later, his son fell from one of the horses and broke his leg. On hearing this news, the villagers rushed to his house.

One of the villagers remarked, 'You were right once again. The ten horses did not prove to be a blessing after all! Your son broke his leg while trying to ride one of them. Now there is no one to help you.'

The old man said, 'Please don't draw any conclusions. We don't know if this is good or bad.'

The villager got upset. 'How can anything good happen from a broken leg? You are crazy!'

The old man said, 'Let us wait for a few days. Who knows, the broken leg may prove to be a blessing in disguise.'

A few weeks later, war broke out in the kingdom. Since the

village was very close to the bordering kingdom, the security was increased immediately. All the young and healthy men were forced to join the army and fight the war. The old man's son was not considered because of his broken leg. The villagers gathered around the old man and cried, 'How right you were! Our sons were forced to go to the war. They will all be killed. You are so lucky. Your son's injury has proved to be a boon for you.'

The old man replied, 'Don't draw such conclusions, and assume that your sons will get killed. The war has just begun. They might lose or win the battle. They might be killed or might survive and be rewarded for their bravery. Only time will tell.'

We make similar predictions in our everyday lives too. We are experts at drawing conclusions about others with very limited information about them. In fact, we are quick at drawing conclusions when we notice a seemingly bad event happening in our friend's or colleague's lives. We swiftly predict what is going to happen next.

On similar lines, when we find our friend or colleague undergoing a good phase in his/her life, we immediately conclude how lucky he/she has been. We are neither willing to look at the hard work put in by the person nor do we wait to see how things unfold for him/her.

We exhibit such traits with the limited information we have. When we are plagued by an unfortunate incident, we are ready to write ourselves off. We love to indulge in self-pity and tell the whole world how unlucky we have been. Similarly, when we are riding on success, we do not realize that the situation can be reversed quite suddenly.

Team Spirit

*Help one another; there's no time like the present and
no present like the time.*

—James Durst

Once, a speaker at a conference gave each participant an inflated balloon. He asked them to write their names on the balloon and hand it over to him. After each participant gave him a balloon with his/her name written on it, the speaker went to the adjacent room and dropped it on the floor. Fifteen minutes later, all the balloons were transferred to the adjacent room.

The speaker announced, 'Ladies and gentlemen, I would like each one of you to go to the adjoining room, pick up the balloon with your name on it, and return to this room within the next ten minutes.'

No sooner had the speaker announced this, all the participants rushed to the adjoining room. Since the door was narrow, there was a mad rush to get inside. Each participant tried to jostle and push the others. Among the few of them who managed to enter, there was a stiff competition to identify their respective balloon. The scramble resulted in total chaos. The situation was no different among the participants who had not been able to enter the room.

What was the result? At the end of ten minutes, not a single person had found his/her balloon. Each one had fought with the rest of the participants and was sulking. The speaker once again asked the participants to go to the adjoining room but with a different set of instructions.

'I would like all of you to enter in a single file. Please pick up the balloon closest to you and hand it over to the person whose name is written on it.'

What was the result now? Within minutes, everyone had his/her balloon. It was not just that. What was noticeable was a drastic change in the atmosphere. Suddenly, each person seemed to be thanking the person who had handed over his/her balloon.

The speaker asked, 'Can anyone explain what happened?'

One of the participants remarked, 'After the first announcement, each one of us wanted to grab our own balloons and return to the room within the stipulated time. However, after the second announcement, we had to hand over the balloons to the rightful owners.'

The speaker smiled, 'You are just stating the facts. What did you learn?'

Another participant remarked, 'During the first phase, the competition was so unhealthy that none of us got our balloons. It was a lose-lose situation for all. Those who managed to enter the room were sulking and upset at the people who had pushed them. And those of us who could not enter the room felt defeated and demotivated.'

The speaker nodded his head, 'That's correct. What about the second part of the assignment?'

The participant replied, 'We followed a strict lane discipline so each of us could enter the room. Since we had to hand over the balloons to the rightful owner, there was teamwork and collaboration that built a healthy team spirit. The atmosphere also remained cheerful. Each participant appreciated the person who had handed over their balloon.'

The speaker clapped his hands in appreciation and said, 'All of you are very quick learners. You have grasped the problem and the solution. Whatever you have observed and learned just now, isn't it a representative of our everyday life too? Everyone is searching for his or her own happiness. There is very unhealthy competition and no one is happy. However, when we give happiness to others, we find our own happiness.' In today's competitive world, what is the most common behaviour that we exhibit? Isn't it to rush towards your targets, even if it is at the cost of others?

One of the biggest changes brought about in the performance appraisal system was the introduction of the bell curve. One of the pioneers of this system was GE's Jack Welch, and it soon became the most popular method for ranking and rating employees. Ranking the employees using the bell curve starts with the assumption that employees' performance follows a normal distribution, something that might not be true in all cases. Many companies that followed this system would fire the bottom 5 per cent or 10 per cent. Though in the initial years, this system led to improved performances, very soon the employees began to work the system. They either fudged numbers to appear good on the assessment scale or began achieving their goals at the cost of others. In an era where the last people were on the firing line, there was an unhealthy scramble to reach the top—a situation similar to the one described during the initial part of the aforementioned anecdote.

A few years ago, many companies around the world realized the inherent flaw in this system. They found out that not only were they losing good people (who were 'force-fit' into the bell curve with a lower rating), but they were also suffering because of lack of teamwork.

So, for a healthy competition among their employees, many companies have now introduced collaborative goals that foster enhanced teamwork. The logic being—an organization that has its employees working towards a common team goal is much more productive and achieves better results. This scenario can be seen in the second part of the anecdote. Rather than asking each person to pick up his/her balloon, the task assigned was to hand over the balloon to its rightful owner.

This is not only true about the corporate world but is also something that happens around us in our daily life. Bengaluru has the dubious distinction of having one of the worst traffic jams in the country—something that gets aggravated due to the innumerable potholes across the city. Have you ever wondered about the root cause of these traffic jams? The truth is they are seldom due to a breakdown of one of the vehicles. In majority of the cases, it is because of poor lane discipline. Everyone seems to be in a hurry to reach his/her destination and, in the process, breaks all rules of lane discipline. I believe that if all vehicles followed a strict lane discipline, every one of us would reach our destination much earlier.

Many years ago, I used to work for a manager who seemed quite aggressive and task-oriented but, in reality, she was of a nurturing kind. She used to set challenging and aggressive targets for each one of us. This made us highly task-oriented and focused on our goals. She was aware that the drawback of this could be failure of teamwork and collaboration. Realizing this, she would always caution us, 'Achieve your goals, but don't leave dead bodies behind!'

It is high time we look at not just our balloons but others' too!

Looking at the Bigger Picture

*If you just focus on the smallest details,
you will never get the big picture right.*

—Leroy Hood

The beautiful archipelago of Lakshadweep Islands lies to the west of the picturesque state of Kerala. Kadmat is one of the most charming islands of Lakshadweep. Pristine beaches border the entire town. This stretch of the Arabian Sea is unpolluted and the colour of the water is aquamarine. Sitting on the sands of the beach and watching the ferocious waves during high tide can be both a spiritual and an exhilarating experience.

One sunny afternoon, a small wave was bobbing in the sea and enjoying itself. The waves were moving at a very slow pace, appearing almost stationary. This little wave enjoyed the sensation of its body moving up and down, as if it was sitting on a seesaw.

As hours passed by, the orange sun began to sink across the horizon. Soon, twilight set in. In no time, the sea began to experience a high tide. The waves began to move towards the shore at a brisker pace. As the waves moved towards the shore, they increased in size and became more ferocious. Watching this, the small wave got excited. It was filled with pride.

'Soon I am also going to become huge and ferocious,' it thought haughtily.

It also noticed the gigantic waves beating noisily against the rocks.

'I too will beat those demonic rocks soon,' the little wave thought.

However, as the little wave approached the shore, it noticed something terrible. Though the sea waves were gigantic and ferocious, they were no match to the rocks. The moment the waves crashed against the boulders, they were vanquished and ceased to exist.

The little waved screamed, 'Oh my God! Look at those poor waves.'

A huge wave passing nearby asked, 'What is the matter? Why are you looking so scared?'

The little wave pointed at the huge waves crashing against the rocks and said, 'Soon, I, too, will be destroyed like them.'

The bigger wave smiled and asked, 'Are you worried?'

'Aren't you?'

The bigger wave laughed and replied, 'No, I am not. Remember, we are not the waves. We are the sea.'

'What does that mean?' the little wave asked.

'When we crash on the rocks, we don't die. We are reborn within minutes and once again gain our full stature. It is a continuous cycle that goes on till eternity.'

Looking at the bigger picture is something that does not come naturally to many of us, neither do we think of a long-term vision. Sometimes, I feel there is a correlation between the two. Those leaders who have a sound long-term vision are able to look at the bigger picture and vice versa. The converse is also true—people lacking in long-term vision are seldom able to look at the bigger picture.

In the above parable, the small wave was initially full of zest and enthusiasm since it found itself increasing in size and ferocity. However, it soon noticed what was happening to the bigger waves that reached the shore. It was terrified that it would also soon crash against the hard rocks and get smashed to bits. It was depressed that all its efforts to gather size would be futile. This happens to us quite frequently in our professional lives as well. During the initial years, we find ourselves on a fast growth mode. Exciting salary hikes, ego-boosting designations, meetings with important clients, and travel across the globe—we are flying high, just like the small wave. However, a few years later, we face a mid-life crisis. As years pass by, the salary hikes reduce and promotions are hard to come by. People much younger than us are now in the limelight. We feel like dinosaurs when it comes to the latest technology—like the small wave watching its future crash against the nasty rocks. Luckily, for the small wave, a veteran wave came to its rescue. It asked the small wave to look at itself as the gigantic sea and not just as a small and insignificant wave. The moment the small wave identified itself with the entire sea, it underwent a complete transformation.

Most people need such mentors when they enter a mid-life crisis. The mentor should know how to make them look at the bigger picture; he/she should be someone who says that the organization is more important than the individual. We should understand that an organization's goals, such as turnover, revenue, share value, customer and employee satisfaction, are our goals because we are the organization.

Knowledge Without Wisdom

Vanity can easily overtake wisdom.
It usually overtakes common sense.

—Julian Casablancas

Once there lived four friends in a small village. When they turned eighteen, their fathers asked them to go in search of a guru who could impart useful knowledge to them. The four boys set out for the journey on foot. During their journey, they shared many things—food, thoughts, ideas, etc.

After a couple of days of walking, this group happened to pass through a thick forest. In the jungle, they came across a crossroads. They discussed among themselves which path to take, but each boy seemed to prefer taking a different direction and there was no consensus among them. Finally, one of them suggested, 'There are four of us and I see four roads ahead. Let each one of us take the road we like to find a guru. Exactly a year from today, let us meet at this junction again and share our experiences.'

'Good idea!' chimed the others in unison.

Saying this, the four boys took different paths and separated from one another. Each of them found a guru and trained well under his guidance. Days turned into weeks and weeks into months. Finally, it was time to reunite. Each boy took leave from his guru and travelled towards the crossroads. Exactly one year later, the four boys reached the predetermined junction. After hugging each other and exchanging pleasantries, they decided to share their experiences over lunch. One of them pointed at a tree and suggested, 'Let us sit in the shade of that banyan tree.' The others agreed and followed him.

As they were about to sit for lunch, they noticed bones of an animal scattered on the ground. The first friend exclaimed, 'Just the thing I wanted to see! Bones of an animal. In the past one year, I spent most of my time studying bones of different animals. My guru taught me how to assemble bones of an animal and convert them into a skeleton. Let me show you all how to do it.'

He sat on the ground and began to reassemble the bones. A few moments later, he had joined all of them. His friends complimented him on his newly acquired skill.

'This seems to be the skeleton of a huge animal,' the second friend remarked.

The first friend nodded his head in agreement, 'You are right. This is the skeleton of a lion.'

The second friend replied proudly, 'Now I will show you what I was taught. I have learnt the art of reciting mantras, and I can easily put flesh on a skeleton.'

Saying this, he sat on the ground in meditation. He closed his eyes and chanted a few mantras. Within a few minutes, the lion's skeleton was covered with flesh. His friends complimented him.

He opened his eyes and pompously said, 'Look, it is now a proper lion. It just needs life and it will be as good as a real one.'

The third friend stepped forward and said, 'My guru taught me to put life into dead animals. If I recite my mantras, we will have a majestic lion standing in front of us.'

The first and second friend patted him on the back and said, 'That's fantastic! Go ahead and put life in the lion.'

'Wait!' shouted the fourth friend.

The other three looked at him in amusement.

'Wait!' the fourth friend repeated. 'Don't do such a foolish thing!' he added.

'Foolish? Who is being foolish here?' the third friend asked.

The fourth friend explained, 'If you put life into a lion, he will obviously kill and gobble all of us!'

The first friend asked, 'What did you learn during the past one year?'

The fourth friend replied, 'I learnt common sense.'

His other three friends laughed. 'Looks like you have wasted the entire year. Common sense, eh?' the second friend guffawed.

'You are jealous of my knowledge, aren't you?' accused the third friend.

The fourth friend cried, 'No, no, no! I am neither jealous nor have I wasted my one year. I am just trying to put some sense in all of you.'

The third friend looked at him sternly, 'No, you are not putting anything into us. I am putting life into this poor creature.'

Saying this, he went and sat near the lion. The fourth friend shouted, 'Wait! Before you start your mantras, let me go and find a hiding place.'

The other three laughed at him.

'Coward!' they teased him.

However, the fourth friend did not bother about their remarks. He quickly climbed the banyan tree and sat on one of its branches. Moments after the third friend had begun chanting the mantras, the lion slowly came to life. It first yawned casually, as if it had been sleeping all along.

'Look, the lion is yawning!' exclaimed the first friend.

'We have succeeded in bringing him to life!' exclaimed the second.

The third friend continued chanting his mantras. Soon, the lion woke up, roared loudly, and looked around hungrily. It noticed the three young lads standing in front of it. In a flash, it pounced on the three helpless boys and killed them. The fourth friend helplessly watched the lion devouring his friends.

◈

If trying to 'add value' to a task without sufficient knowledge is risky, using knowledge without thinking of the consequences can be equally fatal. The above anecdote of the four friends is quite a well-known story.

I remember reading this story in my childhood. Halfway through the tale, the kid in me had marvelled at the skills gained by the first three friends. Just imagine, the ability to assemble bones into a skeleton, add muscles and blood to the bones, and, finally, inject life into a lifeless body! I always wished to have such a skill. After reading half of the story, I had felt sorry for the fourth friend who did not seem to have learnt anything equally fascinating. However, once I had finished reading the entire story, my perception of the four friends had changed drastically. I realized that the first three friends were fools who had used their powers without thinking about the possible consequences. They might have gained knowledge, but they certainly did not have wisdom. The fourth friend, though he appeared to have learnt nothing, eventually turned out to be the wisest of them all.

When the third friend injected life into the wild beast, they had reached a point of no return. The only option for the three of them was to flee from the scene, but since they had not foreseen the threat, they never did. The fourth friend was not only wise but also far-sighted. He was able to judge the gravity of the situation and managed to escape from the lion's clutches. In our lives too, we venture to perform certain foolhardy tasks without realizing the consequences. That can lead to disastrous results.

Acknowledgements

I would like to thank my family for giving me the space and time to write this book. Without their care and sacrifices, it would have been impossible. While other families would shop and watch movies during the weekends, my family would stay back at home to watch me pound my laptop's keyboard.

I would like to thank the team at Rupa Publications for turning my dream into reality—Rudra Sharma, the commissioning editor, for having faith in my manuscript and selecting it for publication, Aparna Kumar, who did a fantastic job of editing my manuscript, and Mugdha Sadhwani for the catchy cover design.

Thanks are also due to Suhail Mathur of The Book Bakers, who helped me in getting the contract with Rupa.

References

http://www.brainyquote.com
http://www.quotegarden.com
https://en.wikipedia.org
http://academictips.org
http://www.attitudeisaltitude.com
http://spears.okstate.edu/home/simkins/quotes/some_of_my_favorite_quotes.htm
http://rishikajain.com
https://maxlucado.com
http://www.citehr.com
Ancient Vedanta